CW00433225

Hidden Streams

A New History

of

Dún Laoghaire–Rathdown

HIDDEN STREAMS

A NEW HISTORY

OF

DÚN LAOGHAIRE–RATHDOWN

BRIAN MAC AONGUSA

CURRACH
PRESS

ACKNOWLEDGEMENTS

Many of the maps and illustrations in this book have come from the author's own collection but he is particularly indebted to various institutions and friends who have most kindly given their permission to reproduce the following in this publication:

The National Library of Ireland for the map *The County of Dublin* (p 90); the illustrations of Dundrum Castle (p 65), Bullock Castle (p 64), Kilgobbin Tower House (p 77), Monkstown Castle (p 93) (from *Beranger's Antique Buildings of Ireland*) and Blackrock Main Street (p 131), as well as the painting (pp 116-117) of the Embarkation of King George IV from Kingstown Harbour.

The Royal Society of Antiquarians of Ireland for the drawings of the Viking symbolic grave markings (p 51); the Royal Irish Academy for the drawing of a *rath* or ringfort (p 30) and the Irish Manuscripts Commission for the *Civil Survey* (p 88).

Pádraig and Moira Laffan for photographs of Brennanstown and Kilternan megalithic tombs (pp 17 and 20), Dalkey Island (pp 24–25) and Tully West Cross (p 32).

Rob Goodbody for the photograph of the surviving Pale ditch near the Ballyogan Recycling Centre (p 80).

Conall and Sally Mac Aongusa for the painting of Kingstown as viewed from Dalkey Hill Quarries (p 141).

Liam Clare for the photograph of the Ring at Lehaunstown Races (p 142).

Matt Fitzgibbon for the photograph of Bray Harriers at Cabinteely (p 145).

The Irish Times for the photograph of flooding at Rathfarnham (p 156).

Oxford University Press for the picture of Viking implements (p 45).

First published in 2007 by
CURRACH PRESS
55A Spruce Avenue, Stillorgan Industrial Park,
Blackrock, Co. Dublin

www.currach.ie
1 3 5 4 2

Cover by Bluett
Layout and artwork by Richard Parfrey
Printed by Estudios Gráficos Zure, Bilbao, Spain

ISBN: 978-1-85607-950-1

LIST OF MAPS AND ILLUSTRATIONS

MAPS

ILLUSTRATIONS

Contents

BUÍOCHAS

I am indebted to the Department of Geography at University College Dublin and, in particular, to Professor William Nolan, Dr Arnold Horner and Dr Séamas Ó Maitiú for inspiring and guiding me in the fascinating field of historical geography.

I have drawn heavily on previous research, especially by Christiaan Corlett and Peter Pearson, and also on in-depth local research undertaken by Rob Goodbody, Liam Clare, Liam Mac Cóil and the late Kathleen Turner.

Two local history groups – the Foxrock Local History Club and the Kilmacud Stillorgan Local History Society – also deserve my special thanks for providing continual stimulation at their meetings and outings, and for giving me opportunities to speak to them about local rivers and streams.

This book would not have emerged in such an elegant and attractive format without the professional publication skills of Currach Press, in particular of its editor Jo O'Donoghue and layout designer Richard Parfrey. To both of them I express my heartfelt thanks for their dedication in ensuring that the highest possible standards would be achieved in the presentation of this book.

Mar fhocal scoir, tá mo bhuíochas ó chroí ag dul dom bhean chéile Máire, a chuir ar mo shúile tábhacht na Sean Ghaeilge mar fhoinse eolais agus a thug tacaíocht leanúnach dom fad is a bhí an leabhar seo á scríobh.

Brian Mac Aongusa
Lúnasa 2007

PREFACE

The sound of a running stream always fascinates. If hidden from view, it becomes even more fascinating. Where does the stream come from, where is it going and why does it sometimes disappear from view?

Seeking answers to such questions can lead to the discovery of a people's history back to the earliest times. The history of Dún Laoghaire–Rathdown has been deeply influenced by many of its rivers and streams, of which there are about thirty in the county. Indeed, it could be argued that much of the population settlement, as well as the modern shaping of the county, have largely been determined by its watercourses.

By tracing the significance of rivers and streams in the lives of the first prehistoric inhabitants, the early Christians, the Vikings and the Anglo-Normans, this book throws a new light on many of the monuments and landscape features that are still visible today. A study of early maps of the county from 1685 onwards reveals a fascinating world of water-powered industries, side by side with the growth of the first township suburbs of Kingstown, Blackrock, Killiney and Ballybrack, and Dalkey.

In the twentieth century the unrelenting growth of Dublin's southern suburbs has severely impacted on the landscape and character of the county, causing many of its small rivers and streams to be smothered by developments that have driven them underground, or out of sight or even out of memory, like the stream or brook described by Robert Frost in his poem 'A Brook in the City':

The brook was thrown
Deep in a sewer dungeon under stone
In fetid darkness still to live and run–
And all for nothing it had ever done
Except forget to go in fear perhaps.
No one would know except for ancient maps
That such a brook ran water.

This book seeks to unlock a fascinating new history of Dún Laoghaire–Rathdown viewed from the author's historical and geographical perspectives, as well as from his own deep interest in our ancient rivers and streams.

Gur móide ár dtuiscint agus ár meas ar
an bhfód as ar fáisceadh sinn.

That our understanding and appreciation of
our historical roots be enhanced.

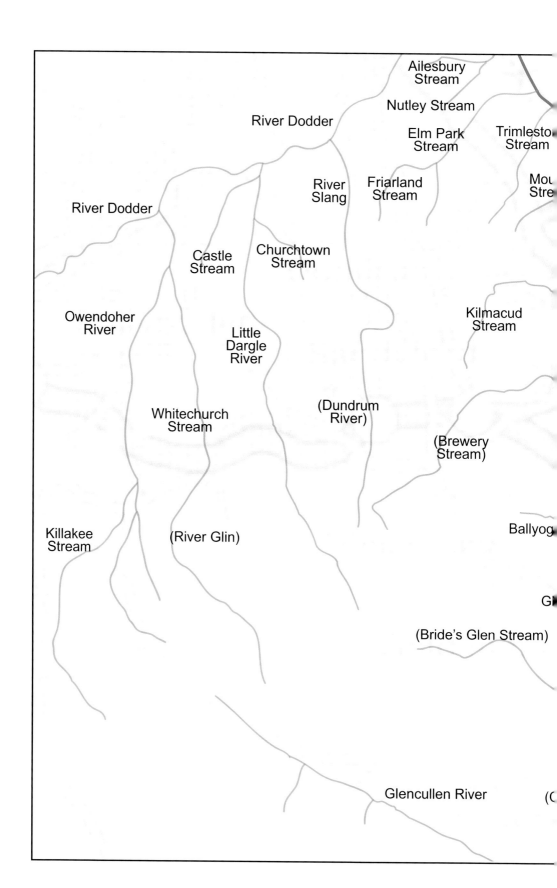

MAP A: RIVERS AND STREAMS
OF DÚN LAOGHAIRE–RATHDOWN

Merrion

Priory
Stream

Glaslower
(Maretimo
Stream)

Stradbrook

Rochestown
Stream

Glasthule

Thomastown
Stream

Dalkey
Island

St Bride's Stream

ıcecourse Stream

Dean's Grange
Stream

Stream

Shanganagh
River

amuck Stream

Loughlinstown River

ınty Brook)

Wood Brook

Fassaroe
Stream

– 1 –

RIVERS AND STREAMS IN PRE-HISTORY

The modern administrative county of Dún Laoghaire–Rathdown
has a prime situation on the east coast of Ireland. Protected by the
Dublin Mountains from the worst excesses of Atlantic storms, it
enjoys a relatively mild climate, rich well-drained soil and good
communications, as well as accessible sandy beaches, an indented
rocky headland and a fascinating small island. Viewed from the
sea, Dún Laoghaire–Rathdown presents a very attractive setting.
No wonder then that the first people to arrive here over 5000 years
ago decided to settle on that small and secure island of Deilginis or,
as it became known much later to the Viking raiders, Dalkey.

MESOLITHIC AGE

The earliest inhabitants of Dún Laoghaire–Rathdown were known
as Mesolithic people. These were primitive hunters, fishers and
gatherers, who led a subsistence lifestyle from day to day without
engaging in any farming. They lived in the Stone Age, using a
stone technology of crude flint instruments. Though a very hard
stone, flint can be worked by chipping to create a razor-sharp edge
suitable for a wide range of domestic and hunting implements.

Archaeological research has shown that these early people
lived on a mixed diet that included wild pig, red deer, salmon,
trout, eels, sea fish, shellfish, woodland and coastal birds, as well

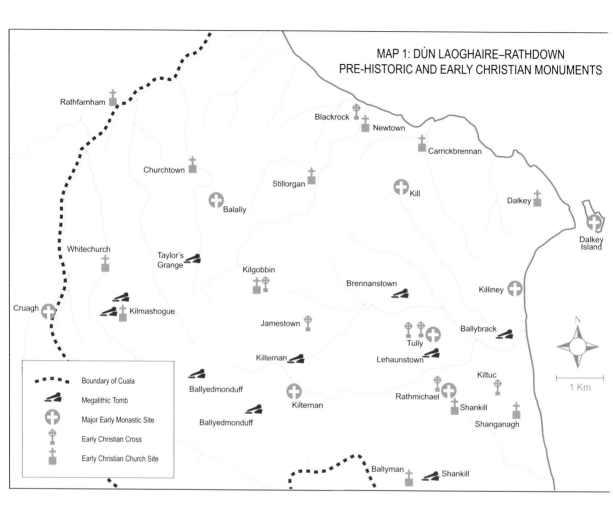

MAP 1: DÚN LAOGHAIRE–RATHDOWN
PRE-HISTORIC AND EARLY CHRISTIAN MONUMENTS

Rathfarnham

Blackrock
Newtown
Carrickbrennan

Churchtown

Stillorgan
Kill
Dalkey

Balally

Dalkey
Island

Whitechurch
Taylor's
Grange
Kilgobbin
Brennanstown
Killiney

Cruagh
Kilmashogue
Jamestown
Tully
Ballybrack

Kilternan
Lehaunstown

Kiltuc

Ballyedmonduff
Kilternan
Rathmichael
Shankill

Ballyedmonduff
Shanganagh

N

1 Km

Boundary of Cuala

Megalithic Tomb

Major Early Monastic Site

Early Christian Cross

Early Christian Church Site

Ballyman
Shankill

as the fruits of the forest. They were a nomadic people who built only temporary dwellings, usually small domed huts of timber stakes, covered in deer hides or turves. They carried all their possessions with them, including their deer hides, which could be re-used in the construction of their next dwelling.

The latest archaeological research, based on radiocarbon dating techniques, reported by local archaeologist Christiaan Corlett, suggests that Dalkey Island was inhabited around 3340 BC.

Important evidence found there includes flint stones and large collections of discarded seashells, known as middens, as well as a selection of fish, bird and animal bones, illustrating the diverse diet of the first inhabitants of Dún Laoghaire–Rathdown. Using the secure island as their base, these Stone-Age people made forays into the adjoining mainland then densely covered by woodlands ranging from hazel scrub to tall forest trees, including oak, pine, elm and ash. Most probably, these early people used the rivers and streams to penetrate the unknown interior in search of subsistence. In this way, they gradually moved further inland to discover other suitable locations for their hunting, fishing and food-gathering.

Brennanstown megalithic tomb near the Ballyogan Stream

Significantly, small numbers of flints have been found along the coast at Dún Laoghaire, as well as inland on the Shanganagh River at Loughlinstown and on the River Dodder at Rathfarnham. These finds, which are on view in the National Museum in Dublin, indicate that there were small groups of Mesolithic people living on the coast and also inland along rivers and streams. A midden has been discovered in the bend of the River Slang near Dundrum and some flint implements have been found near Cruagh and Tibradden along the Owendoher River and the Whitechurch Stream. Clearly rivers and streams provided essential routes for the Mesolithic people that enabled them to become the first to discover Dún Laoghaire–Rathdown.

NEOLITHIC AGE

The practice of farming reached Ireland around 3000 BC, having developed in the Middle East and gradually spread across Europe. The farming way of life introduced by the Neolithic people did not immediately replace the earlier hunting, fishing and gathering lifestyle. Both lifestyles existed side by side for some time, but more and more people began to try to control their food supply with the aim of providing a surplus for use during the leaner times of the year. To achieve this aim the Neolithic people began to open up the landscape by removing some of the woodland areas to create fields for planting food crops. Animals were domesticated both to provide a food supply and to give protection against hidden dangers, such as wolves, bears and wild boars lurking in the surrounding forests. The cultivation of cereal crops and the maintenance of cattle required people to settle rather than wander and this led to the first permanent settlements along the rivers and streams, as well as along the coastline.

In this new economy new technology evolved. Stronger stone axes were developed to remove the trees, pottery was manufactured to provide storage for food and querns were made of stone to grind corn. Because of people's dependence on the weather and good fortune for their essential needs, new religious practices evolved and greater importance was given to honouring the dead. The early Neolithic farmers built enormous stone tombs for their dead and some good examples are still to be found in Dún Laoghaire–Rathdown. These large tombs were known as megaliths and a study of their locations, detailed in Appendix I, gives us an insight into the distribution of the earliest Neolithic settlements. Most are in close proximity to a river or stream and are built along the flanks of the Dublin Mountains or further down the valleys but always close to running water. As shown on Map 1 (p 16), those facing west lie in the steep upper valleys of the Owendoher River, Whitechurch Stream and Little Dargle River, while those facing east are downslope, extending almost into the lowlands at Kilternan on the Loughlinstown River, at Brennanstown on the Ballyogan Stream and near Ballybrack on the Shanganagh River. The earliest farmers must have had particular regard for rivers and streams, certainly as a source of water for domestic and farming use but also perhaps for religious reasons, equating continuity of life with running water.

A study of items excavated by archaeologists at megalithic monuments gives us some idea of the society in which these articles were used. Stone tools were found at many of the monuments, as well as domestic pottery, stone arrowheads, scrapers, knives, axe heads and querns for grinding cereals. At the massive Kilternan tomb, distinctive hollow scrapers, designed perhaps for the preparation of arrow shafts or for reaping, have been excavated. The finding of arrowheads, typically leaf or lozenge shaped, indicates either that hunting was still important for food supply

Kilternan megalithic tomb with capstone weighing over twenty-five tonnes

or that frequent warfare had developed in early Irish society. It is of interest that several examples of arrowheads have been found during archaeological excavations at Kilternan, Taylor's Grange, Whitechurch, Rathfarnham and Carrickmines, as well as on Dalkey Island. Many of these are on view in the National Museum in Dublin.

Megalithic tombs were the first permanent structures built in Dún Laoghaire–Rathdown and are important in that they reflect the first attempts made by settled people to organise the landscape around them. The tombs highlight divisions within Neolithic society, as they were probably built to mark the burials of important and highly esteemed leaders, rather than those of the builders themselves. Principally they served as tributes to those buried within but were also probably used as ceremonial religious centres for the people who built them and lived nearby. Several different forms of megalithic monuments were built in Ireland by the Neolithic people but the most common type in Dún Laoghaire–Rathdown is the *portal tomb*, so-called because of the portal or door-like entrance. The portal stones support a dramatic roof stone, which often rests on a smaller stone at the rear of the tomb. The roof, or capstone, of the massive Kilternan tomb is estimated to weigh over twenty-five tonnes. How the earliest farmers, using only stone technology, managed to lift such capstones on to the supporting stones remains a mystery. The term *dolmen* is also used to describe these monuments. It derives from the Breton *daul maen* or table stone.

BRONZE AGE

After 2000 BC the techniques of smelting copper ore reached Ireland from the European mainland. Copper cakes were produced that could be melted down and poured into stone moulds to produce metal daggers or axes. Flat copper axes were the most common products of this new technology and examples of them have been found in Dún Laoghaire–Rathdown at Dalkey, Cabinteely and Glencullen. Over time metal workers learned to mix tin with copper to produce bronze; this formed a more rigid blade than that made with copper alone. This further development in technology gave birth to the Bronze Age, a period that continued for some 1500 years until about 600 BC. Sophisticated implements from this period have been discovered; among the articles found were a fine copper rapier excavated at Killiney Hill and a palstave weapon taken from a pool in the River Dargle near Bray.

The megalithic tradition continued for some centuries into the Bronze Age, but tomb construction changed. The new type, known as the *wedge tomb*, had entrances facing west in the direction of the setting sun. Burial sites also varied considerably between 2000 and 1600 BC. Ashes from cremations and skeletons were buried in a range of tombs and were often accompanied by, or even contained within, specially designed pottery. Some were *cist* burials, placed within stone-lined graves or in simple pits dug in the ground. In Dún Laoghaire–Rathdown archaeologists discovered a cemetery of such burials at Edmondstown on the Owendoher River, where a range of funerary pottery was found. However, like most Bronze Age burials, they were not marked by any sort of monument. Nowadays such burials are usually found by chance as a result of ploughing, quarrying or excavation works. In 1955 a *cist* burial found beside the Obelisk at Stillorgan

PASSAGE GRAVES

♦ Among the most famous monumental tombs built in Ireland are the passage graves of *Brú na Bóinne* in the Boyne Valley at Newgrange, Knowth and Dowth. Lesser known, but also striking, are the passage graves of *Sliabh na Cailli* on the Lough Crew Hills near Oldcastle, County Meath. These types of tombs take their name from the stone passage that leads to a burial chamber within a large circular earth and stone mound. Inside the burial chambers are splendidly wrought historic motifs with spirals, lozenges and zig-zags at *Brú na Bóinne* and extraordinary floral designs at *Sliabh na Cailli*.

An important series of passage graves stretches across the west Wicklow and south Dublin Mountains. The easternmost example, a small collapsed passage grave known as Fairy Castle, is located on top of Two Rock Mountain or *Sliabh Gearr*, just behind Three Rock Mountain or *Sliabh Rua*, overlooking Dún Laoghaire–Rathdown. As most of the county until relatively recently consisted of many agricultural farms, it is likely that farmers working their lands over the past 5000 years would have been familiar with this megalithic monument which is visible as a small lump, or stone cairn, on the top of Two Rock Mountain. ♦

Park contained the disturbed remains of the skeleton of an adult female, whose death was apparently caused by a sacrificial blow to the skull. Other Bronze-Age *cist* burials have been discovered in the lowlands along the Glaslower at Stillorgan and the Dean's Grange Stream near Kill-of-the-Grange.

Towards the end of the Bronze Age from 1200 to 600 BC – a period associated with mythological tales, with primitive Irish language and with Queen Maebh, Cúchulainn and the famous saga of *Táin Bó Cuailgne* or *The Cattle Raid of Cooley* – metal workers with the aid of clay moulds developed high skills both in bronze and gold. During excavations on Dalkey Island a large number of clay mould fragments were found, indicating an important metal-working production site, particularly of socketed axeheads and spearheads. Such axes have been found, for example, at Rathfarnham, Stillorgan and Ticknock. This was a time of rising wealth, as reflected in the discovery of two gold personal ornaments near Rathfarnham on the Owendoher River and near Monkstown on the Carrickbrennan Stream. A spearhead found at Rathmichael near Shankill would suggest a new concern with weaponry at a time of rising wealth. The hillside site of Rathmichael, enclosed by a large defensive rampart, was a significant fort and probably represented a focus of some political importance in Dún Laoghaire–Rathdown around 1000 BC.

IRON AGE

Archaeologists consider the Bronze Age to have ended around 600 BC, giving way to a new period known as the Iron Age that continued until the arrival of Christianity around AD 400. This was the time associated with Fionn Mac Cumhaill and his band of warriors *Na Fianna*, whose adventures were related to St Patrick and his scribes and consequently absorbed into Irish folklore. Several monuments from the Iron Age, such as standing stones and hill forts, have been identified in Dún Laoghaire–Rathdown. The function of standing stones is uncertain. They could have been used to mark burials, boundaries or routeways. There are still standing stones to be seen in Glencullen and beside the road from Marlay Park to Rockbrook. Both Rathmichael and Tully are likely sites of hill forts and evidence of defensive promontory forts has been found near the mouth of the Glaslower at Blackrock and on Dalkey Island.

Aerial photography and recent excavations in Dún Laoghaire–

Rathdown have shown that there was some settlement of the interior, as well as along the coast, during the Iron Age. Although it was most likely a thinly distributed population compared to later periods, the general concentration of significant monuments in the area is evidence of a strong presence of inhabitants in Dún Laoghaire–Rathdown throughout the prehistoric period. Mouths of rivers and streams along the coast provided the earliest inhabitants with the means of exploring the interior. Archaeological finds suggest that the first people on Dalkey Island began to explore the River Dargle near Bray and the Shanganagh River system from Killiney Bay to Loughlinstown and beyond. In Dublin

Dalkey Island, first inhabited around 3340 BC according to latest evidence

Bay the Carrickbrennan Stream, the Glaslower and the River Dodder and its tributaries were explored to reach the interior as far as the foothills of the Dublin Mountains. In pre-historic Ireland, rivers and streams provided the first pathways for the exploration and early cultivation of the area now known as Dún Laoghaire–Rathdown.

Iron Age Mythology

Although asociations with Dún Laoghaire–Rathdown have not been preserved in Early Irish folklore, one of the earliest stories written from Leinster mythology is the eighth-century tale *Togail Bruidne Da Derga,* or 'The Destruction of Da Dearg's Hostel'. It concerns Conaire Mór, a mythical king of Tara, whose escapades led him to places located close to Dún Laoghaire–Rathdown. This makes it the earliest story ever written about the county.

Togail Bruidne Da Derga describes how Conaire Mór's father, Eterscéle, who was of royal stock, had no issue until he married a young girl, Mess Buachalla, who had been abandoned by her parents. This girl had been impregnated by a man from another world who came to her in a bird-skin. The spectre had told her she would give birth to a son and 'that boy may not kill birds and Conaire shall be his name'. The young Conaire was sent into fosterage in *Magh Life,* probably the Curragh of Kildare, and when he grew to early manhood his father, Eterscéle, died. Conaire was then summoned to attend a bull-feast at Tara, which involved a seer sleeping on a bull-hide in expectation of a vision which would reveal who of royal stock should be the new king. He set out in his chariot and on his way Conaire saw some huge unusual white-speckled birds and pursued them as far as the sea near *Áth Cliath,* or Dublin. There the birds took off their skins and, taking human form, told him of his *geasa* or prohibitions that included being forbidden to cast a stone from his sling at birds. Conaire was further instructed to take great care not to transgress any of his *geasa*, but to go naked to Tara where he would be installed as king.

Meanwhile, the seer at the bull-feast had a vision 'of a naked man coming along the road to Tara at dawn, bearing a stone in his sling.' Conaire came to Tara in this fashion and his fosterers met him on the road and clothed him with royal garments. When inaugurated as king, Conaire Mór adopted as his motto 'to enquire of wise men so that I myself may be wise'. Conaire Mór's reign ushered in a period of great happiness and good fortune in Ireland. His three foster-brothers, however, were jealous of him and began to ravage and plunder. Conaire Mór was loath to punish them and, out of love for them, refused to put them to death, but banished them to Scotland. Unwittingly, he had then broken several of the *geasa* which the bird-men had imposed on him when they told him he was to be king.

Years later, when Conaire Mór was travelling one night on the ancient road of *Slighe Chualann* by the River Dodder on the northern boundary of Dún Laoghaire–Rathdown, he decided he would visit the hostel of his old friend Da Dearg, which was probably located near the place now called Bohernabreena or *Bóthar na Bruidhne*, meaning the hostel road. Riding ahead of him along the road, Conaire Mór perceived three horsemen making for Da Dearg's hostel. They wore red tunics and red mantles, carried red shields and spears, rode red horses and they were red-haired. Conaire Mór remembered that one of his *geasa* was against following three red men into the house of Dearg. He then asked Lé Fer Flaith, his son, to pursue the three horsemen and persuade them not to enter in advance of the king, but Lé failed to overtake them. They always remained a spear-cast ahead and so entered Da Dearg's hostel. Resigning himself to his fate, Conaire Mór then entered the hostel and the three red men sat down with him. A woman with a horrible-looking face came to the door and foretold that 'neither hide nor hair of you will escape from this house, save what the birds will carry off in their claws'.

Meanwhile, his three foster-brothers with three fifties of boats had landed from Scotland at *Trácht Fuirbthen*, or Merrion Strand, with five thousand marauding Britons. They marched inland towards the hostel in the foothills of the Dublin Mountains and launched a surprise attack but Conaire Mór with three fifties of warriors managed to kill hundreds of the foe. The raiders then set fire to the hostel three times, but each time the conflagration was quenched by the defenders. Then druids who were with the raiders put a magic thirst on Conaire Mór and although the *Dothra*, or River Dodder, flowed through the house, not enough water could be found to quench the king's thirst. His champion, Mac Céacht, was sent for water to *Tipra Cuirp* in *Crích Chualann*, an unidentified well somewhere in Dún Laoghaire–Rathdown, but he could not find enough water there.

Meanwhile, Conaire Mór grew weaker and weaker until finally he was slain by two of his foe. The mythical tale ends in describing how Conaire Mór's severed head spoke a verse in praise of his champion Mac Céacht, who unfortunately returned too late with a supply of water to save his king.

$-2-$

The Coming of Christianity

Christianity brought to Dún Laoghaire–Rathdown a range of intellectual and technological advances that transformed the landscape. Central to this transformation, which began some time after AD 400, was a very large increase in population and farming across the area then known in Gaelic Ireland as the *tuath* of Cuala.

Cuala

From the sixth to the ninth century the area extending from the River Dodder southwards to the Glen of the Downs and Delgany in modern County Wicklow and eastwards from the Dublin and Wicklow Mountains to the sea constituted the small kingdom of Cuala, ruled by the dynasty of Uí Briúin (O'Byrne) Chualann. It is quite remarkable that the boundaries of that ancient Gaelic kingdom, which were determined largely by rivers and streams, still form most of the boundaries of the modern county of Dún Laoghaire–Rathdown. The River Dodder and the Castle Stream form the greater part of the northern boundary, and the Owendoher River mainly forms the western boundary of the modern county, as in the *tuath* of Cuala. Much of the southern boundary of the modern county was fixed by the Fassaroe Stream and the River Dargle, when the smaller southern part of Cuala was transferred

to the new County Wicklow when it was formed as the last county
of Ireland in 1606.

The *tuath* of Cuala enjoyed a measure of security and
prosperity in the Early Christian period. Because of the protection
afforded by the Dublin Mountains from the kings of *Laighin*
centered at Dún Ailinne near Kildare and of the distance of the
tuath from the strong kingdom of *Brega* centered at Knowth on the
River Boyne, the people of Cuala were able to develop relatively
stable political and social structures. But the early written history
of Cuala seems largely to have been ignored by early chroniclers.
Its many churches are rarely mentioned and its political leaders
in secular society receive scant attention. Glimpses of life during
this period may be gleaned only from some interesting references
to Cuala in Early Irish texts. One in particular states that a person

Reconstruction of
a *ráth* or ringfort
by Deri Warner

30

who does not consume the mead (honey drink) of Cuala is not suitable for kingship. Another refers to a tradition that the area of Dún Laoghaire–Rathdown in the ancient Gaelic world was famous both for its milk and its mead, which were consumed from vessels made from the horns of wild oxen. A further tradition concerning the first smelting of gold in Ireland relates that the artificer was named *Uchadán* of Cuala. This attraction to milk, mead and gold suggests that an affluent society was living in the area of Dún Laoghaire–Rathdown in the Early Christian period.

SECULAR SOCIETY

Surviving written records combine with archaeological evidence to give us a better understanding of a more highly organised society after the coming of Christianity. The two main elements of that society were the monastic church and the secular population, whose chief economic pursuits were the acquisition and exploitation of dairy cattle. Between AD 600 and AD 900 the population was housed within earth or stone enclosures known as *ráthanna* or ringforts, which partially defended the possessions of wealthy farmers. Within the *ráth* the farmer built his timber house, typically round in plan. Some of the smaller farm animals may have been kept within the enclosure and several excavated sites have shown that metal-working, glass-making and other craft industries like textile manufacture also took place within the *ráth*.

The frequency with which the word *ráth* occurs in modern Irish placenames gives an indication of the significance of these Early Christian secular settlements. Archaeological studies show that the distribution of surviving *ráth* sites is extensive within Dún Laoghaire–Rathdown, with numerous examples to be found on the east-facing slopes of the Dublin Mountains. It is significant that

many of these sites occupy the better drained hill slopes above the 200m contour, suggesting that large farmers preferred to live in locations from which they could keep a close eye on their cattle in the lands below.

MONASTIC CHURCHES

In contrast, the monastic churches were located in the valleys of the rivers and streams. Most probably, they were near important arteries of communication and consequently became focal points for the local communities. In Dún Laoghaire–Rathdown there were no fewer than seventeen monastic churches during the seventh and eighth centuries. They were housed within enclosures large enough to accommodate urban functions, such as markets, industries and education. Scholars consider some monastic sites to have been of major importance because of evidence found of an enclosure, a round tower, a high cross or intricate stone carvings. They have concluded that eight of the Early Christian monastic sites in Dún Laoghaire–Rathdown were of major importance and were in fact service centres for the surrounding population. Early Christian churches and crosses are listed in Appendices IIA and IIB. An important and previously unknown site of an Early Christian cemetery was recently uncovered during reconstruction work on a service station on the N11 at Mount Oliver just south of Cabinteely. Over 1500 skeletons were found in this fifth- to twelfth-century burial site, together with many artefacts indicating a relatively wealthy society engaged in trade, craft production and agriculture.

It will be seen from Map 1 (p 16) that the locations of the eight major monastic sites were spread across the county, suggesting a fairly even distribution of population between the sixth and ninth

Twelfth-century West Cross at Tully with figure holding crozier

33

centuries. Evidence of these major sites still survives in varying degrees and this evidence merits attention before the sites become further obscured by ever-encroaching development.

RATHMICHAEL / *RÁTH MHÍCHIL*

A lane on the left of the Rathmichael road leading from the present Church of Ireland building to Ballycorus reaches this attractive major site high on the eastern slope of Carrickgollagan. The ancient small church stands on a height in the middle of a graveyard, the whole of which is enclosed by a rampart of earth and stone. This rampart is what remains of the great hillside Iron Age fort that originally occupied the site. Its large size suggests that it must have belonged to a chieftain who gave it to a holy person so that a church could be built within it. The remains of this Early Christian church may be seen and at its southwest corner may be found the base of a round tower some two metres high. The tower has been dated to the ninth century and is proof of the importance of this major monastic site. The name of Rathmichael was first mentioned in AD 1179 in a papal bull listing churches in the diocese of Dublin. Unusual gravestones with symbolic markings, known as Rathdown *leaca*, were first discovered here in the nineteenth century.

TULLY / *TULACH NA NEASPAG*

A minor road to the left of the Cabinteely to Carrickmines road some 500m beyond Cabinteely village leads to the other major hillside site of Tully, known in Irish since very early times as *Tulach na nEaspag* (The Mound of the Bishops). The impressive ruins of the twelfth-century church include a graceful Romanesque chancel arch in perfect order, as well as round-arched windows. In a field on the other side of the road from the church is a twelfth-century high cross depicting a bearded figure of a bishop in full-length garment holding a crozier. On a plinth in the roadway is another plain wheel cross, possibly from the tenth century, undecorated except for a shrine-type cap badly weathered. The site, according to legend in the fifteenth-century *Book of Lismore*, was founded by or closely associated with St Brigid of Kildare, whose name it bears. As St Brigid died in AD 523, this major monastic site could go back as far as the sixth century. It was mentioned in the papal bull of AD 1179 as *Tullaghnanepscop,* granted to the Augustinian Priory of the Holy Trinity in Dublin. Early gravestones with unusual symbolic markings of the Rathdown *leac* type have also been found at this Early Christian site.

DALKEY / *DEILGINIS*

In the old graveyard at the northern end of Dalkey's main street, adjoining the Goat Castle Town Hall, is the ancient eleventh-century church first recorded during the thirteenth century as *Kilbegnet.* A holy woman, St Begnet, is believed to have founded the Early Christian churches both in the town and on Dalkey Island. The ruins of the Dalkey church are quite substantial, with three doorways and seven windows still intact. An Early Christian cross is incised into the exterior wall. Clearly it was a sophisticated church in the Middle Ages, when Dalkey was an important port handling trade for Dublin. The graveyard surrounding the ancient church has also yielded an early gravestone with symbolic markings of the Rathdown *leac* type, which is displayed at the adjacent Dalkey Castle and Heritage Centre.

Early Christian plain
high cross, possibly
tenth century, at Tully

The ancient tenth-century church on Dalkey Island, dedicated also to St Begnet, is a good example of an Early Christian church with a square-headed doorway and extended side walls. Unusually high walls suggest an apartment or loft to accommodate a priest, probably during stormy weather in winter when travel to the mainland might not be possible. There is an early cross carved on the rock face opposite the doorway of the church. Access to the island today is possible by the boat service from Coliemore Harbour during the summer season.

KILLINEY / CILL INÍON LÉINÍN

On Marino Road leading east off Killiney Hill Road lies this site containing an ancient, possibly sixth-century, church first mentioned in the papal bull of AD 1179 as *Cellingenalenin*, believed to commemorate the seven holy daughters of Léinín. One of Léinín's daughters, Aiglend, had a son, Fintan, who may have been the founder of the monastic church at Kill, or Kill-of-the-Grange as it is known today. Trees and houses now almost obscure the Killiney site and the enclosure that once encircled it. But this ancient Early Christian church has an arch with inclined jambs and a typical doorway wider at the base than at the top. The west doorway has a Greek cross carved on the underside of its lintel, a sign that scholars believe may indicate that this monastic site was dedicated to nuns. The only other example of a similar carving on the underside of the lintel of a west doorway may be seen at Our Lady's Church in Glendalough.

KILL / *AN CHILL*

A little to the north of Clonkeen crossroads and beside the Dean's Grange Stream lies the major tenth-century site of Kill, first

Early Christian church at Rathmichael, first mentioned in the 1179 Papal Bull

♦ Irish placenames are generally a good guide to the identification and location of Early Christian churches. If the placename includes *kil, sti* or *ta* in its prefix, it is likely to indicate a church of the period dedicated to the person usually named in the suffix. For example, Kilgobbin near Stepaside means the church of the Welsh saint, Gobban; Stillorgan means the place of the Irish saint, Lorcan; and Taney means the house of Nahi, a seventh-century monk from the famous monastery of St Maelruain at Tallaght.

The name of the founding saint or associated holy person has in some cases faded from public memory, but notable names have survived. St Mochuda, who was baptised by the sixth-century St Brendan, reputed to have discovered North America by way of Iceland, is commemorated in Kilmacud near Stillorgan; the fifth-century St Tuca, grandson of Senac, chief of *Críoch Cualann*, is honoured in the name of Kiltuc near Shanganagh Castle; and Killegar near the Scalp probably commemorates a Welsh St Adgar.

The ruling dynasty of the *tuath* of Cuala in the Early Christian period, the Uí Briúin Chualann, originally came from Kildare. Under the strong influence of the famous monastery founded there by St Brigid, they promoted devotion to the saint throughout Cuala. As a consequence, strong associations with St Brigid have survived to this day in Dún Laoghaire–Rathdown. Not only is the monastic site at Tully near Cabinteely still dedicated to St Brigid but her memory is preserved in modern names such as Bride's Glen near Loughlinstown, Kilbride above the River Dargle near Bray, St Bride's Stream running through Cornelscourt and Cabinteely, and the Church of Ireland Parish of Stillorgan named in honour of St Brigid. ♦

mentioned in the papal bull of AD 1179 as *Cluinchenn*. A very small Early Christian church was founded here in the sixth century by St Fintan, but was considerably extended in later centuries to serve the growing population of the surrounding fertile lands. What remains today is the substantial ruin of an eleventh-century church complete with bellcote and an arch in the east gable. The church, which belonged to the Augustinian Priory of the Holy Trinity in Dublin, stands in an ancient graveyard surrounded by a high wall in the middle of modern suburban housing.

KILTERNAN / *CILL TIARNÁIN*

In a cul-de-sac off the Kilternan to Glencullen road stands this major site on high ground, which falls steeply to a stream that becomes the Loughlinstown River. The plain twelfth-century church ruin, whose founder has not been established with any certainty, is surrounded by an ancient graveyard. Inside the church is a *bullaun* stone used in baptismal rites. The owner of the surrounding lands in the Middle Ages was Domnall Mac Gillamocholmóg. A Rathdown *leac* was also found at this major site.

BALALLY / *BAILE AMHLAIDH*

The remains of this site lie some two kilometres south of Dundrum in the private grounds of the Central Bank of Ireland. The ruin suggests an ancient church but little is known of its early history. There is no apparent connection with an Irish saint, as the site is associated with a Norse name Olaf, or Amhlaidh in Irish. Balally, as all modern Luas travellers will know, is *Baile Amhlaidh* or the place of Amlaíb (Olaf). In the papal bull of AD 1179 there is a reference to *Ballyvroolef*, which presumably meant this ancient Early Christian site.

CRUAGH / *CRAOIBHEACH*

The ancient cross of Blackrock

A short distance from Rockbrook on the road to the Pine Forest above the Owendoher River is a modern cemetery, which has been added to a much older one containing the slight remains of an ancient church. Its founder has been traced in the *Tripartite Life of St Patrick* to Dalua of *Craoibech,* described as being 'of Patrick's household'. The *Martyrologies of Tallaght and Donegal* refer to a Dalua *Tigi Bretan*, described as 'a pilgrim of the Britons and one of Patrick's household'. *Tigi Bretan*, or the place of the Britons or Welshmen, is of course Tibradden Mountain above this ancient site. The name *Craoibech*, meaning a branchy place, over time became Crewagh leading to the modern name of Cruagh.

It is interesting that, of these eight Early Christian sites of major importance, four are located near rivers or streams. Cruagh is above the Owendoher River, Balally is near the Dundrum River, Kilternan is above a stream that becomes the Loughlinstown River and Kill is beside the Dean's Grange Stream. Two others, Dalkey and Killiney, are at coastal sites, while Tully and Rathmichael are hillside sites overlooking the Shanganagh and Loughlinstown River valleys.

Blackrock's Ancient Cross

♦ At the south end of the Main Street, at the junction of four roads, is a modern plinth on which stands the ancient cross of Blackrock. Its origin is uncertain, although it probably belonged to a forgotten church in the locality or it may have marked at some time the boundary between churches. It is known that the Byrne family of Cabinteely were its custodians in recent centuries. The small cross is about 75cm high and 60cm wide across the arms, has a human head on the shaft on one side and what appears to be some sort of ring or circle decoration on the other. It has been suggested that this cross may be the oldest of the freestanding crosses in Dún Laoghaire–Rathdown.

From medieval times, the cross was used as an important landmark, indicating the outer limit of the boundaries and jurisdiction of the city of Dublin. Jurisdiction was affirmed once a year in an imposing ceremony known as the *Riding of the Franchise* during which 'the Lord Mayor and Corporation of Dublin accompanied by members of the various City guilds, on horseback, with trumpeters, etc, all in holiday attire, rode round the bounds of the City Liberties.' Descriptions exist of this ceremony as far back as 1488 and again in 1603. The boundary of city jurisdiction was a line coming down the lane of the old Merrion churchyard, beside the Tara Towers Hotel, and 'running along the centre of Rock Road as far as the Cross of Blackrock, thence in a straight line to the sea, extending out to sea as far as a man could wade at low water and cast a javelin'. A map in the National Library of Ireland, published by Scale in 1773, shows the *Black Rock* in the sea due north of the *Old Cross* and a dotted line indicating the route taken in the ceremony of *Riding the Franchise*.

Within living memory, the ancient cross was much revered by old residents of Blackrock village. Funerals coming from the church of St John the Baptist first headed north along Temple Road as far as the cross, where the cortège would pause for a short while before retracing its steps to the church and then continuing south to Dean's Grange Cemetery. ♦

Although most of these major sites can be referred definitely to periods earlier than AD 900, it is not always possible to give even an approximate date for the ancient churches. The founders of the majority of them were either unknown or little known people who led a holy life devoted to the practice of religion or asceticism. The Early Christian churches were built to a plan of the utmost simplicity, usually consisting of one small rectangular chamber measuring about nine metres by five and a half metres, or less. The masonry of these churches shows a very high standard of skill, with the largest stones often of enormous size placed at the base. In some cases the side walls project as much as thirty centimetres beyond the gable ends and it is thought that this may have been copied from older churches built of wood.

There is much evidence to suggest that the first Christian churches were of timber construction and that stone may not have been used extensively until the ninth century. The Venerable Bede of Northumbria writing in his eighth-century *History of the English Church* refers to the churches of the Irish as being 'made of hewn oak and thatched with straw'. Further evidence of wooden construction is the fact that in Early Irish a church was commonly known as *dairtheach* or house of oak. In places where trees were scarce – such as Dalkey Island – stone was used from the outset to build churches in Early Christian times.

It should be noted that churches in the this period were individual in character, each ruled by an abbot and completely independent of one another. There was no central church authority at that time. Only in the twelfth century was the concept of a unified hierarchical church applied in Ireland, as had already been done in other parts of the Christian world.

Other noteworthy characteristics of the Early Christian

churches were a door in the west end, instead of an arch, with a massive straight stone lintel and inclined jambs, with a tiny window at the east end often providing the only light. These tiny churches, solidly built with large stones and standing as if their feet were apart, projected an air of permanence and strength. They were starkly devoid of any architectural ornament, but scholars suggest that their inner gloom may well have been illuminated by the gleam of gold and coloured jewels from the sacred vessels used in religious ceremonies. As may be seen from Map 1 (p 16), many small churches of this kind were built all over Dún Laoghaire–Rathdown, almost invariably in the valleys of small rivers and streams or at coastal sites.

– 3 –

THE VIKING INFLUENCE

In the margin of a famous ninth-century manuscript, the St Gall copy of Priscian's Latin grammar, an unknown scribe wrote the following verse in Old Irish:

> *Is acher in gáith innocht*
> *Fo-fuasna fairggae findfolt.*
> *Ní ágor réimm mora minn*
> *Dond láechraid lainn ua Lothlind.*

> (The bitter wind is high tonight
> It lifts the white locks of the sea.
> In such wild winter storm no fright
> Of savage Viking troubles me.)

FIRST VIKING RAIDS

These few short lines written in the ninth century graphically reveal the frightening prospect of a Viking raid. Monks living on Rathlin Island off the north Antrim coast were the first in Ireland to experience the onslaught of these Scandinavian raiders, when their monastic settlement was burned and ransacked in AD 795. Three years later, when the Vikings raided Inis Pádraig off Skerries on the north Dublin coast, they took away as plunder the rich

Display of
Viking domestic
implements
discovered
in Dublin

44

shrine that contained the relics of St Mochonna, associated with the twelfth-century church of Carrickbrennan near Monkstown in Dún Laoghaire–Rathdown. The initial impact of these raids was as ferocious as it was sudden and unexpected. The widespread fears felt throughout Ireland at that time were comparable to those experienced following the 9/11 terrorist outrage in New York in 2001.

For decades after these first hit-and-run attacks, Vikings in their longboats attacked monastic settlements along the coasts of Ireland with devastating effect. These monasteries were targeted for plunder by the Vikings – just as they had previously been attacked by Irish kings – because they were considered to be places of safe-keeping for treasure and monastic wealth. In a raid down the east coast in 821, a monastic settlement at Howth was targeted when the Vikings 'took a great prey of women', presumably from a nunnery there. In 836 they attacked the monastic settlement at Glendalough, moving inland from the coast at Arklow and through the Avonmore valley over thirty kilometres of difficult terrain. The following year, the first Viking fleet consisting of sixty ships entered the mouth of the River Liffey and began substantial raiding in the midlands destroying *cealla, dúne, treba*, (churches, forts and homelands) according to the annals.

The year 841 saw an important new development that had long-term implications for Dún Laoghaire–Rathdown. A Viking *longphort* or naval camp was established at the mouth of the River Liffey, from which attacks were directed not only against the interior of Ireland but against other targets along the length of the Irish Sea. As their concentration was still on larger and wealthier monasteries, the relatively smaller monastic sites in Dún Laoghaire–Rathdown seem to have been spared in these early Viking raids. With the establishment of the *longphort*, a permanent Viking settlement grew around it and began to exert

46

an influence on the hinterland and its people, which included Dún Laoghaire–Rathdown. Over the following decades the Vikings gained footholds along the coastline and established Norse colonies, including proto-towns at *Vikingaló* (Wicklow), *Veigsfjorthr* (Wexford), and *Vethrafjorthr* (Waterford). These early settlers appear to have come from Norway, as scholars maintain that most of the Norse loan words in the Irish language can be traced to a dialect in south-western Norway.

The second half of the ninth century saw a serious development for the Norse. In 849 a fleet of 120 ships of Danes arrived in Irish waters. They clashed with the earlier settlers and eventually routed them in a great three-day naval battle on Carlingford Lough in 853. These Danes, referred to in the annals as *Dubgall* (black foreigner) to distinguish them from the Norse *Finngall* (fair foreigner), have left their mark on Dún Laoghaire–Rathdown through the many people with surnames of Doyle or MacDowell, and also on north Dublin with the placename of *Baile Dubgall* or Baldoyle, as well as the modern name of Fingal for its administrative area. The Danes, however, soon fell victim to dynastic feuds and when Dublin divided into two camps, their power began to ebb. In 902 the Irish kings of *Brega* to the north and of *Laighin* to the west joined forces and decisively defeated the Danes to bring an end to the first Viking settlement of Dublin.

SECOND VIKING AGE

The second Viking Age began suddenly in 914 with what the annals describe as 'the arrival of a great sea-fleet of pagans in Waterford Harbour'. This fleet was led by Ragnall, who was called *rí Dubgall* or king of the Danes because he ruled Danish Northumbria. He took control of Viking activities in Ireland and, joined by two leaders of the Danish dynasty exiled from Dublin, began renewed attacks and war against Irish kings. Within three years, the Vikings had retaken Dublin and Ragnall then sailed to north Britain where he led campaigns that made him king of York and ruler of Northumbria. York and Dublin were now ruled by a single dynasty and Ragnall was called *rí Finngall 7 Dubgall* or king of the Norse and the Danes. This new mixed Scandinavian kingdom, which he and his successors ruled, enhanced the importance of Dublin and had long-term political and cultural consequences, including an influence on Dún Laoghaire–Rathdown. Under a succession of Danish kings, Dublin grew to become a real power in the north Irish Sea, the Isle of Man, the Hebrides, Scotland and northern England. It was a sea-kingdom, the centre of economic and political interests, and it had formidable resources. Located on the western shore of the Irish Sea at a point where the northern trade routes passed from Scandinavia, the Faroes and the Hebrides down to England and continental Europe, Dublin had a pivotal role in the development of Viking trade and commerce in the tenth and eleventh centuries.

As an international trading centre, not unlike the International Financial Services Centre in modern Dublin, the Viking settlement at the mouth of the Liffey generated prosperity and wealth that extended into its hinterland. Dún Laoghaire–Rathdown benefited from boat-building and repair, grain growing and milling, as well as the growing of food crops to support Viking Dublin. Viking names that have survived provide evidence of this, for example: Bullock Harbour (*Blowick* in Old Norse) the old boat-building facility, Balally (*Baile Amlaíb*) near the Norse-named River *Slang* through Dundrum, where grain milling probably took place, *Dalkey,* a literal Norse translation of the original Irish name Deilginis, and the name of Rathmichael that appears to represent a dedication to St Michael, who was the patron saint of seafarers among the Norse.

Dún Laoghaire–Rathdown, as a service area for Viking Dublin which probably had a population in the thousands by the tenth century, developed closer ties between its indigenous population and that of the international trading town. Evidence from the annals shows that commercial and cultural contacts, intermarriage and the spread of Christianity among the Vikings made relations easier with the Irish. There is ample evidence of intermarriage and fosterage from as early as the tenth century. The most famous example was Gormlaith, daughter of Murchad Mac Find, king of Leinster, whose three marriages became the subject of this amusing verse preserved in the genealogies:

> *Trí lémend ra-ling Gormlaith,*
> *Ní lingfea ben co bráth:*
> *Léim i nÁth Cliath, léim i Temraig,*
> *Léim i Cassel, carnmaig ós chách.*

> (Three buck-leaps were made by Gormlaith,
> which no other woman shall do until Doomsday:
> a buck-leap into Dublin, a leap into Tara,
> a leap into Cashel, the plain of mounds above all.)

This verse refers to the ability and agility of Gormlaith in first marrying Amlaíb Cuarán, Viking king of Dublin, then marrying Maél Sechnaill Mac Domhnaill, high king in Tara, and finally leaping into the bed of the Munster king Brian *Bóraime* or Boru, to whom she bore two sons. Clearly, the Gaelic and Scandinavian cultures existed side by side in tenth-century Ireland.

The Viking Amlaíb Cuarán, whom Gormlaith first married, was described by the English chronicler Florence of Worcester as 'the pagan king of the Irish and of many islands'. During his reign from 945 until 980, Amlaíb Cuarán intervened in Welsh dynastic disputes, drew slaves and tributes from Wales and plundered it. His sons, raiding from Howth and Dalkey, pillaged Holyhead and the Llyen peninsula, bringing back many slaves. The annals also record much plundering of Irish monasteries during the period. This caused such anger that the Irish kings began to resent the foreigners and sought to capture Dublin. Finally Maél Sechnaill Mac Domhnaill, high king of Tara and Gormlaith's second husband, inflicted 'a very great slaughter on the foreigners' and captured Dublin in a decisive battle in AD 980.

It is very significant that the victor of that battle made no attempt to destroy the city nor to expel its occupants. For the next century and a half, Irish kings preferred to see the 'foreigners' of Dublin as a source of wealth and tribute. Rather than seeking to have 'foreign power ejected from Ireland' as claimed in certain propaganda annals, the various pretenders to the high-kingship of Ireland were vying with each other to achieve effective control over the wealthy settlement of Dublin. The so-called achievement of Gormlaith's third husband, Brian *Bóraime* or Boru, in expelling the Vikings from Ireland after the battle of Clontarf in 1014, was simply an invention of the O'Brien dynasty to advance their claim to the high-kingship of Ireland. Based on the facts, scholars have rejected the concept of the battle of Clontarf as a national victory over the Norsemen. In reality it was more of a spectacular episode than a decisive landmark in the history of the Scandinavian occupation of Ireland.

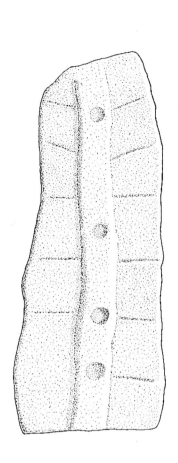  

CULTURAL INFLUENCES

During both the Viking and subsequent Irish control of Dublin the entire surrounding region undoubtedly prospered. The very size of this international trading centre required regular provision of labour, foodstuffs and building materials from the farms, pastures and woodlands of Dún Laoghaire–Rathdown. This brought prosperity to the county and there is important evidence from this period that wealthy Vikings lived there, converted to Christianity and encouraged the growth of many existing church foundations,

Various Viking symbolic grave markings found in Dún Laoghaire–Rathdown. The central *leac*, from Rathfarnham, shows a saltire cross.

as well as the construction of several new churches. They also had erected on their graves distinctive headstones that have not been found elsewhere in Ireland. This type of gravestone is known today as a Rathdown *leac* (meaning flagstone, and pronounced *le-yak*). Since the nineteenth century a total of twenty-five *leaca* have been found in Rathmichael, Ballyman, Killegar, Dalkey, Tully, Kilgobbin, Kilternan, Whitechurch and Rathfarnham. The widespread occurrence of Rathdown *leaca* in a large number of ancient graveyards in Dún Laoghaire–Rathdown illustrates the extent of Viking settlement and indicates their influence on local churches in the area.

Viking *leac* or grave-slab at Rathmichael

As may be seen from the illustrations, the Rathdown *leac* features a distinctive type of decoration not found elsewhere in Christian Ireland. No two *leaca* are the same, but there is generally a repetition of motifs. The most common decorations include a herringbone design and cupmarks, often enclosed by concentric circles, and are based on local Viking art styles. The decoration on a *leac* frequently does not fit into the range of Christian symbols, but the meaning of any special symbolism has been lost over time. When a cross features on a *leac* it generally takes the form of a saltire cross, shown in the illustration from Rathfarnham (p 51), which is so elongated that it is no longer recognisable as a cross. Early antiquarians argued that the *leaca* were pre-Christian but today they are generally regarded as having been influenced by Viking art styles and as representing the burials of local Viking chiefs who had converted to Christianity before 1000.

LANGUAGE

A positive influence of the Vikings was their cultural and economic interaction with the Irish, which is best seen in areas of commerce and language. The areas of profoundest influence were those of seafaring, farming and urban living. Many modern Irish nautical and fishing terms go back to Norse words borrowed into the language during the Viking period: for example, *ancaire* (anchor), *bád* (boat), *stiúir* (rudder), *trosc* (cod) and *scadán* (herring). The modern Irish terminology of farming and everyday urban life is even more indebted to the Vikings, for example, *garrdha* (field), *pónair* (bean), *sráid* (street), *fuinneog* (window), *stól* (stool), *bróg* (shoe), *cnaipe* (button) and *margadh* (market). Irish forms of Old Norse personal names began to appear early in the ninth century, attesting to the closer ties emerging between the 'foreigners' and the Irish. By the tenth century, Irish aristocrats were borrowing some of these names, especially the usual royal names among the Viking leaders, such as Amlaíb, Ímar, Sitric and Ragnall. The last is still preserved in the modern Irish surname of Reynolds. The Vikings borrowed Irish names a little earlier and by the eleventh and twelfth centuries there were many with purely Irish names. This shows that deep intermingling had taken place between the Vikings and the Irish long after the 'foreigners' had supposedly been driven out of Ireland in 1014.

But the greatest influence of the Vikings on Dún

Laoghaire–Rathdown was probably the new era of international communications they introduced. No longer were its inhabitants solely concerned with the politics and problems of neighbouring small Irish kingdoms. Now they were being exposed to new external cultural, social and economic changes that would broaden their horizons and extend their knowledge of the outer world. This invaluable experience of the Viking 'foreigners' would be of great benefit to them in coping and assimilating with the next wave of 'foreigners' shortly to arrive and occupy the county of Dún Laoghaire–Rathdown.

VIKING SLAVERY

A less savoury influence attributed to the Vikings was the growth of slavery and in particular the development of a lucrative slave trade at Dublin, operating from a prison camp on Dalkey Island. From the ninth century, the taking of slaves was an integral part of Viking warfare. It was never the prime motive for raiding but was a means of indicating defiance and was followed up by the extraction of ransom and tribute. In the eleventh century, when the internal struggle for *ard rí* or over-kingship escalated in Ireland, it became clear that the Irish had learnt from the Vikings. The taking of slaves became a widespread phenomenon in Ireland and warring Irish kings sold their prisoners of war in Viking Dublin's slave-market. The city experienced a booming slave trade with Scandinavia, Western Europe and Iceland in the tenth and eleventh centuries.

The first recorded instances of Vikings taking large numbers of captives from slave raids in Ireland occurred after 880. When the monastery at Kildare was attacked in 886 it was recorded that 280 persons, including the prior, were led to the Viking ships. The

Annals of Ulster record a major slave-raid on Armagh in 895 when no less than 710 prisoners were taken. Scholars consider that these examples of ninth-century slave raiding were extreme expressions of defiance and bravery for the king, or would-be king, of Viking Dublin. Another objective of the growing number of slave raids was probably the demand for labour in the new Viking settlements of the North Atlantic, including the Orkneys and Iceland. Icelandic scholars have estimated that almost a quarter of the population of Iceland in 930 was of Irish origin. Many of these would have been slaves from Ireland – mostly women and child slaves rather than men, who would be taken only if they had specially needed skills.

From the Irish annals we know only the general outline of the practice of Viking slavery but this outline is paralleled in the Frankish annals for the ninth century. Although there are no written records of Irish slave camps, a very interesting account may be found in the *Miracles of St Benoit* written about 875 in France. This describes a Viking slave camp on an island in the River Loire, comparable to the one operated by the Dublin Vikings on Dalkey Island. This is how the Viking slave camp is described in the ninth-century Frankish annals:

> In the meantime, they had an island – St Florent-le-Vieil at
> the Loire – organised as a port for their ships – as a refuge for
> all dangers – and they built fortifications like a hut camp, in
> which they held crowds of prisoners in chains and in which
> they rested themselves after their toil, so that they might be
> ready for warfare. From that place they undertook unexpected
> raids, sometimes in ships, sometimes on horseback, and they
> destroyed all the province…

In the tenth century Irish kings began to unite with Viking kings in raids designed to capture prisoners for the Viking slave trade. In 938 king Ceallachán of Cashel united with the Waterford Vikings to plunder the midlands and Meath. They took many prisoners, including the abbots of Clonenagh and Killeigh in Offaly. One of the abbots was evidently led to Dublin and kept imprisoned on Dalkey Island. The *Annals of the Four Masters* for the year 939 record that the abbot of Cill-Achaidh (Killeigh) drowned at Dalkey Island while 'fleeing from the foreigners', but it is likely that he was attempting to make his escape from the Viking prison camp there. His fate gives a poignant insight to the particular horrors of slavery. Having been sold off to Dublin when there was no longer any prospect of obtaining ransom money for him, the unfortunate abbot was being held captive on Dalkey Island for the Dublin slave market when he tried unsuccessfully to swim ashore in a desperate attempt to regain his freedom. The use of a lonely island off the coast of Dún Laoghaire–Rathdown as a prisoner slave camp is paralleled in the account already quoted from the Frankish annals of the island camp of St-Florent-le-Vieil on the River Loire.

THE IRISH ADOPT SLAVERY

After the middle of the tenth century there is evidence that the Irish kings were learning the practice of slave-trading from the Vikings and were even turning this humiliating weapon against them. The annals seem to suggest that the idea of Irish slaves for Irish households was spreading. General social development in Ireland at the time seems to have become degraded and some people were even selling their own children to cope, for example, with debts incurred in a harsh winter. The *Annals of Ulster* record for the year 964:

*Gorta mór díulochta in n-Erind, co renadh int athair a mac 7 a
ingen ar biadh.*

(A great intolerable famine in Ireland, so that the father would
sell his son or daughter for food.)

As a whole, however, there is no evidence to suggest that the
institution of slavery in Ireland, or even in Dublin, was anything
more than a marginal phenomenon of luxury for the nobles.

Irish evidence clearly points to the eleventh century as the
high point of the Irish Sea slave trade. Dublin had become the
foremost trading centre of Ireland, taking over the role of the
great monastic settlements. Other Viking towns like Waterford
and Limerick also became renowned ports and valuable assets
to any Irish king claiming his over-lordship and control over the
distribution of luxury items imported from abroad, such as wine,
silk, handicrafts and precious stones. To buy these articles, the
Irish would have to supply two commodities, cattle and slaves.
Leather and beef were in local demand in cities all around the Irish
Sea and luxury items, such as slaves, were in constant demand by
the aristocrats, whether Scandinavian, Anglo-Saxon or Irish.

There is clear-cut evidence that slavery became more
widespread in Ireland among both the Irish and the Vikings in
the eleventh century. *Lebor na Cert* or *The Book of Rights*, written
about 1100, contains lists of the stipends of the over-kings to the
lesser kings of their domain, together with lists of tributes due from
the lesser kings. While the latter cover hard necessities like cows,
oxen, boars, sows, etc., the over-kings clearly were expected to
bestow goods of extreme luxury, such as horses, ships, shields and
swords, gold and slaves. The descriptions of the slaves are highly
interesting. Female slaves, crudely called *banmog*, are referred

57

to as 'full-grown', 'swarthy', 'fair', 'graceful' and 'valuable'. The Leinster king was obliged to give 'eight women whom he has not dishonoured'. Male slaves are described as 'lads', 'hard working', 'strong-fisted', 'willing', 'expensive' and 'spirited'. Such descriptions indicate that slaves were primarily intended for the household, as servants, concubines, mountebanks or the drabants of the court. *Lebor na Cert* also draws a clear distinction between native and foreign slaves, referring to 'foreigners who do not know Irish' and 'women from over the great sea', suggesting not only that slaves were a product of internal warfare but that some were supplied by foreign trade. Most foreign slaves must have come by way of the Viking cities.

THE END OF SLAVERY

The practice by warring Irish kings of taking Irish people as captives declined after 1115 but it appears that foreign captives continued to be taken. This may explain why the Church Synod of Armagh in 1170 saw the imminent Norman conquest of the Irish as God's punishment 'because it had formerly been their habit to purchase Englishmen indiscriminately from merchants, as well as from robbers and pirates, and to make slaves of them'. The Synod decreed 'that throughout the island Englishmen should be freed from the bonds of slavery and restored to their former freedom'. A clear reference was also made to the 1102 declaration by the Westminster Council of a general prohibition against all trade in slaves in England. Although some illicit trade in slaves in Ireland probably continued afterwards, the Synod of Armagh clearly signalled that the heyday of slave trading in Ireland was well over.

The Vikings brought with them a practice of warfare that had a profound effect on Irish society. Irish weaponry was significantly changed and the Vikings introduced the use of longboats. But they also revived the practice of slavery that had all but disappeared from Irish society since the coming of Christianity. Under Viking influence slavery came to play an important part in Irish military warfare and social life in the eleventh century. Dún Laoghaire–Rathdown also played a significant role in slavery for almost two centuries by having on Dalkey Island a Viking prison camp for Irish and foreign slaves destined for the Dublin slave market.

$-4-$

THE ANGLO-NORMANS

The *Annals of Inisfallen* for 1166 record that Diarmait Mac Murchada, king of Leinster, was 'banished eastwards across the sea after the foreigners of Dublin and the Leinstermen had turned against him.' He made his way to France to seek Henry II, the king of England, who was in his debt since the previous year when Mac Murchada had hired his fleet to the king for his campaign in Wales. After acknowledging Henry II as his lord, Diarmait was given permission to recruit fighting men in England to help him recover his position in Ireland. Mac Murchada found his first recruits among the Anglo-Norman lords in the border lands of south Wales. These lords, led by Richard FitzGilbert – better known in later years as Strongbow – were particularly receptive to Diarmait's promises of new lands in Ireland waiting to be won by the sword.

INVASION AND CONQUEST

Mac Murchada returned to Ireland in 1167 and quickly re-established his position in the south-east with the help of a small body of Anglo-Norman knights. Three years later, Strongbow arrived with a larger force and took control of the Viking-ruled city of Waterford. By way of reward, Diarmait formally gave his daughter Aoife in marriage to Strongbow; the lavish ceremony

is depicted in a large painting by Daniel Maclise (1806–70) on display in the National Gallery of Ireland. Within a few weeks of his marriage, Strongbow and the king of Leinster were marching north with Anglo-Norman forces to take control of Dublin. By that time Dublin had come to replace Tara as the country's symbolic capital. It had the single greatest concentration of economic wealth and had an extensive network of trading contacts overseas.

When the Anglo-Normans arrived, the rulers of Dún Laoghaire–Rathdown were the Gaelic clan of Uí Briúin Chualann or the O'Byrne family. Dublin was ruled by the Mac Torcaill family of Viking descent and a prominent member of that family, Sitric Mac Torcaill, had granted the church at Tully and surrounding lands to Christ Church in Dublin. The Anglo-Norman lords Raymond le Gros and Miles de Cogan led the attack on Dublin and, after a three-day stand-off, the city was finally taken in September 1170. Most likely, it was then plundered by the Anglo-Norman forces led by Mac Murchada and Strongbow.

Example of surviving Anglo-Norman *motte* at St Mullins, Co. Carlow

Henry II arrived in Ireland within a year as he was worried by Strongbow's rapid ascent to power. He granted the kingdom of Leinster to Strongbow but held control of the city of Dublin for himself. In 1173 Strongbow granted an extensive range of lands to a Yorkshireman, Walter de Ridelesford, as a knight's fee for his part in the conquest. Walter was a councillor of Strongbow and was known to his peers as a brave and noble warrior. The territory granted by Strongbow included the kingdom formerly known as Cuala but, when de Ridelesford sought royal confirmation of this grant, Henry II took back much of the land and kept it for himself. However, he allowed de Ridelesford to hold Bray and lands at Glencullen.Lands retained by the Crown included Powerscourt, Ballycorus, Kilternan and Corke, near Bray, which became a royal demesne. One former Gaelic ruler, Domnall Mac Gillamocholmóg, retained his lands south of Bray, principally because of his marriage to Dervogilla, the daughter of Diarmait Mac Murchada, which made him Strongbow's brother-in-law. Domnall submitted to Henry II on his arrival in Ireland in 1171 and was allowed to retain the lands of Kilruddery, as well as his principal residence at Rathdown, near Greystones in modern County Wicklow.

The taking of Dublin by the Anglo-Normans had significant long-term implications for Dún Laoghaire–Rathdown. Within a decade of their arrival, the conquerors had planned and implemented a systematic colonisation of lands held there for centuries previously by the Gaelic clans. Henry II ensured, however, that large areas of Dublin's hinterland would be retained by the Crown and that much of the land in Dún Laoghaire–Rathdown would be reserved for the Archbishop of Dublin and the new European monastic orders. The latter had replaced the system of independent Early Christian churches during the eleventh and first half of the twelfth centuries. The Archbishop of Dublin held on to lands at

Dalkey, Rathmichael and Shankill, while the Augustinian Priory of the Holy Trinity established a manor at Clonkeen on lands it had already held before the arrival of the Anglo-Normans. The Priory also held lands at Killiney, Loughlinstown and Shanganagh. The Cistercian monks of St Mary's Abbey in Dublin established a grange at Monkstown on the Carrickbrennan Stream on land they too had held since before the invasion. The European monastic orders also received land grants from many of the Anglo-Norman lords.

Economic Exploitation

Unlike previous invaders who mainly sought pillage and plunder, the Anglo-Normans quickly changed their emphasis from conquest to economic exploitation. They made a long-term investment in Ireland and expected wealth in return. To achieve this goal they imported the agricultural system with which they were familiar in England, based on the Norman manor and on a mixture of arable and pastoral farming techniques. The Irish-speaking tenants of the previous Gaelic owners, the O'Byrnes, were not removed from the land, but were supplemented by imported English peasants and artisans. At that time land was scarce in England and the promise of new farmland and improved conditions of tenure in Ireland attracted many settlers. Most of them came from the west midlands and the southwest of England, sailing from the ports of Bristol and Chester. The legacy of this movement of people at the behest of the Anglo-Normans may still be found in Dún Laoghaire–Rathdown in common surnames like Bermingham, Stafford, Dowdall and Bruton.

As a result of this colonial movement, much of the landscape of Dún Laoghaire–Rathdown was transformed dramatically in

Bullock Castle,
built originally by
Cistercian monks
from St Mary's
Abbey, Dublin,
in the thirteenth
century to protect
their lands and
fishing rights

the space of a few generations. Countryside woods were cleared, arable cultivation was expanded and internal and foreign trade soared. The city of Dublin enjoyed an extended period of physical expansion, including the reclamation of lands from the wide mouth of the River Liffey. Economic growth, development and prosperity ensued, as exemplified in the splendour of Dublin's medieval cathedrals of Christ Church and St Patrick's, as well as the foundation of several wealthy religious houses in the city. The conquering people had an image of themselves as being chosen by God to civilise the barbaric Irish. Luckily, climatic conditions were in their favour as a sustained period of warmer weather benefited Ireland towards the end of the twelfth and during the thirteenth

The Castle of Bullock, 6. Miles from DUBLIN.

centuries. Perhaps never until the recent advent of the 'Celtic Tiger' at the end of the twentieth century did Ireland experience a transformation and economic boom quite like that of the thirteenth century.

NORMAN MANORS

The Anglo-Norman lords had been attracted to Dún Laoghaire–Rathdown because of its good agricultural land and its favourable situation by the sea. They quickly took possession of the area and began to superimpose the Norman manorial system of landholding

Sixteenth-century ruin of Dundrum Castle, built to replace the first thirteenth-century Anglo-Norman stone castle

Dundrum 3ᵈ view.

on their newly conquered territory. On entering a new territory the Anglo-Normans would first construct a large mound of raised earth with a flat top, surrounded by a fence, and would then build a wooden tower on its summit. This primitive castle, known as a *motte-and-bailey,* could be defended with ease and provided a base from which raids could be made into lands still held by a local Gaelic king. When that king had been finally subdued, the invading lord would then divide the best land in the territory among his own supporters. The lord resided in the manor house and established nearby a village that contained the parish church, the lord's mills, ovens and kilns, as well as the tenants' cottages. The manorial village became the focus of economic life and of law and order, while the parish church became the communal centre of religious activities.

Norman manors were located on good agricultural land and, unlike the *ráthanna* of Gaelic Ireland, none was located above the 200m contour. Almost all were at sites either on or close to rivers or streams. The new lords had a preference for established sites with an existing infrastructure, sites that were adequately connected by road, well supplied with water and having some political significance. An important feature of the Norman manorial system was the close association of manor and church. As may be seen from Map 2 (p 76), many of the identified manors in Dún Laoghaire–Rathdown were located near a major Early Christian church site, often at the centre of a medieval parish. This coincidence between manorial centre and parish church was conducive to enduring settlement.

In the first few decades after the Anglo-Norman invasion the lord of the manor lived on a *motte-and-bailey* structure of earth and timber. Even though it was largely out-of-date in contemporary Europe, the *motte* was valuable in Ireland for both prestige and defence reasons. It elevated the bed and sittingrooms and the halls of the residence above the surrounding land, rendering them highly visible and prestigious. But the primary function of the elevated residence was the protection of the small manorial farmsteads from perceived threats from the dispossessed Irish clans living at the outer edges of the good land taken over by the invaders.

From the thirteenth century, however, the more powerful lords began to build stone castles, while the smaller baronial settlements continued to have the older and more traditional earthwork structures. Scholars believe that *mottes* may even have continued to be used until the fourteenth century when the concept of stone tower houses began to emerge as a better form of defence against the increasingly frequent raids by the dispossessed Irish.

MANORIAL CENTRES

In Dún Laoghaire–Rathdown the locations of seven Norman manorial centres have been identified. Interestingly, four were located near the major ecclesiastical sites from the Early Christian period at Balally, Kilternan, Kill and Dalkey, while two others near Rathfarnham and Kilgobbin adjoined the site of an Early Christian church. The seventh Norman manorial centre was at Cornelscourt on St Bride's Stream, not far from the other centre at Kill-of-the-Grange. All six inland manorial centres were located on rivers or small streams. In addition to the seven identified manorial centres, borough status was conferred on three other Norman manors in Dún Laoghaire–Rathdown. These were in the south-eastern part of the county at Killiney, Connogh and Corke. Scholars believe that this status was probably used to attract Norman settlers to these underdeveloped coastal areas and to entice them to stay. These three manors were also located close to church sites.

A highly organised system of agriculture based both

The Ports of Dalkey

♦ When the Anglo-Norman manor was abandoned at Shankill early in the fourteenth century, the Early Christian settlement at Dalkey began to prosper. At least since Viking times, a port had developed at the natural creek of Bullock, where Cistercian monks from St Mary's Abbey in Dublin had built their first castle early in the thirteenth century to protect their lands and important fishing rights. Throughout the late Middle Ages, Dalkey was used for the transport of people and merchandise to and from England and continental Europe. Most of the land around Dalkey was owned by the Archbishop of Dublin and the principal economic activity of the area was fishing. The archbishop's harbour at Coliemore opposite Dalkey Island and the former Viking harbour at Bullock were both used as ports. Their activity generated income and enhanced the prosperity of Dalkey.

Though not an official port, Dalkey became an alternative port to Dublin, which was precarious for shipping in the fourteenth century due to silting at the mouth of the River Liffey. Ships from England, France and Spain would anchor in Dalkey Sound and offload goods, especially wines, bound for Dublin at Coliemore. They would then be sent to their destination either by land or by smaller craft along the coast. Often, however, ships were only lightened before continuing to Dublin, as the cost of conveying goods by road added significantly to their eventual price. To handle the volume of merchandise passing through Dalkey, merchants in the village built fortified townhouses during the fifteenth century for the safekeeping of goods. Tradition holds that there were originally seven castles in the village but only two of these – Archibold's Castle (pictured right) and Goat Castle – survive today.

Many notable passengers landed at the ports of Dalkey, including John Penros who arrived as Chief Justice in 1384 and Philip de Courtenay as Lord Deputy in 1385. Lord Lieutenants who first landed at Dalkey included Thomas of Lancaster in 1402 and Sir John Talbot in 1414. Probably the most notorious arrival was the infamous Lord Deputy Sir Henry Sydney who landed at Dalkey in 1565. However, by the end of the sixteenth century, Ringsend had been adopted as the port of Dublin and soon after, the importance of Dalkey began to decline. Fishing once again became its main economic activity. ♦

on pasture and cultivation, as well as a totally new system of administration, was introduced by the Anglo-Normans. They built large and imposing residences to oversee their lands, established manors and boroughs with their own markets and currency, and founded several new parish churches. The manor house, the tenants' cottages and the parish church evolved in the thirteenth century into an administrative and social centre for a countryside that was intensively worked both for cattle and food crops. For example, by 1330, wheat, barley, oats, beans and peas were all being harvested at Kill-of-the-Grange. This new system was ruled by Anglo-Norman lay lords or, in the case of church lands, by the Archbishop of Dublin and the new monastic orders.

Archibold's Castle, Dalkey, a fifteenth-century fortified storehouse

This complete reorganisation of Irish life and society was observed with great resentment by the previous Irish landowners who had been driven by the invaders into the marginal lands of the Dublin and Wicklow Mountains. These were the O'Byrnes who formerly ruled Uí Briúin Chualann from Ballytenned, known as Powerscourt today, and the O'Tooles who had ruled from Castlekevin, near Annamoe in modern County Wicklow. It was no surprise that these dispossessed people began to attack the new owners on their former lands and steal their cattle, raid their barns and sometimes destroy their dwellings. For the first period after the Anglo-Norman invasion, lords of the manor lived on a *motte-and-bailey* structure of earth and timber, a form of construction not impervious to serious fire and destruction. Because of this danger, the Anglo-Normans soon began to build stone castles and later tower houses to protect themselves from attacks by those whom they called 'the wild Irish'.

NORMAN CASTLES

Early in the thirteenth century the first Norman stone castle in Dún Laoghaire–Rathdown was built on the *drom* or ridge above the River Slang at Dundrum, in order to consolidate defence against raids by the former Irish owners of Anglo-Norman lands now living in the nearby Dublin and Wicklow Mountains. The second stone castle was built later in the same century on a hill slope near Shankill to help protect lands in the southern part of Dún Laoghaire–Rathdown from raids by the O'Byrnes and O'Tooles. These earliest castles consisted of a keep or *donjon*, which was the main residence of the lord. Around this keep was a courtyard or *bailey,* enclosed by a *bawn* wall within which a garrison of soldiers could be housed.

The castle at Dundrum was unusually fine and, though only an empty shell of a sixteenth-century ruin now survives, it was clearly of considerable strength. To find it, the visitor, if approaching Dundrum from the south, should turn left at the traffic lights in the centre of the village, cross the bridge over the bypass, swing left at the roundabout and turn into a gateway leading to the ruin. It consists of two towers, the thick walls of which rise to some twelve metres, crowned with stepped battlements associated with the sixteenth century. The windows are large and a few of the original loops remain, but the roof has gone. It was thatched originally, but an early nineteenth century engraving shows a slated roof on the impressive castle. The first owner of the land here after the Anglo-Norman conquest was Sir John de Clahull, Marshall of Leinster, but the present ruin is of the sixteenth-century castle built about 1590 by Richard Fitzwilliam to replace the original Norman castle.

The second stone castle was at the Anglo-Norman settlement, known as *Senekyll*, located some two kilometres west of the modern village of Shankill on Ferndale Road in low-lying ground at the foot of Carrickgollogan. A sixteenth-century tower house marks the site but today it is privately owned and inhabited. The original castle was built early in the thirteenth century by Henry de Loundres, Archbishop of Dublin, and it served as the administrative centre of his manor. No description of this castle survives, but a description of the Archbishop's castle at Swords, north of Dublin, in 1326 would probably give an insight into what comprised the manor at Shankill. It depicts a crenellated stone-built house, roofed with shingles, comprising a stone kitchen and larder, a hall and a chamber for friars. Near the gate was a chamber for the constable and four chambers for knights and squires. All were roofed with shingles. The *seneschal* or manorial courts of the Archbishops of Dublin were held in the castle at Shankill up

71

to the mid-seventeenth century.

Despite the construction of these two strategic castles, attacks by the dispossessed Irish continued and the Anglo-Normans were not very successful in resisting them. They did not appear to have any concept of a frontier with the native Irish, making it very difficult for them to prevent unpredictable attacks or defend against them. Another problem was that the Anglo-Norman lords were often absentees, while many of the native Irish had remained working the lands that they or their leaders had previously owned. It became easy for the Irish tenants to revolt against their new landlords, who in their absence could not enforce their rule of law. Gradually the situation got out of control and the Anglo-Norman estates, including those owned by the archbishop and the various monasteries, became unviable.

GROWING INSTABILITY

It was during the Bruce invasion of Ireland in 1316 that the native Irish took advantage of the growing instability of Anglo-Norman rule. The Dublin and Wicklow Mountains became known as the 'land of war' because of the resurgence of the old Gaelic power of the O'Byrne and O'Toole families. They continued for the next 300 years to terrorise the Norman-ruled countryside almost as far as the gates of Dublin. Even the archbishop's manor at Shankill, which was relatively close to the centre of Anglo-Norman control at Dublin, would appear to have been deserted in 1326 when it was described as:

> There are no buildings at Senekyll; once there were but they
> are now burned and thrown down by Irish felons...Certain
> burgagers at Senekyll, holding 17 burgages, used to pay 17s/1d,

but now nothing because they have fled from that country on account of the Irish.

Many of the Anglo-Norman landlords could no longer afford to run their estates and those owned by the archbishop and the monasteries were leased to retainers on condition that they defend them from the Irish. In some cases, the English crown was even forced to take possession of lands and post garrisons of soldiers there to defend them. Eventually, the colonisers realised that there would have to be a frontier between the lands they worked and those still under the control of 'Irish felons'. In 1429 they promulgated the Subsidised Castles Act which provided grants of £10 to encourage the construction of many more castles to defend a frontier between the Anglo-Normans and the increasingly hostile hinterland around the centre of their rule at Dublin. This act gave rise to the building of a considerable number of new castles, known more specifically as tower houses, across the county of Dún Laoghaire–Rathdown.

– 5 –

MEDIEVAL DEFENCES

While the Anglo-Norman occupation of Dún Laoghaire–Rathdown had spread quite rapidly in the latter part of the twelfth century and had become well established in the thirteenth, it did not succeed as a permanent conquest. There is much evidence that the area was under constant threat of attack by the neighbouring Gaelic Irish clans whose incursions resulted in great damage to crops, cattle and other property. The Anglo-Normans soon realised that a medieval castle rooted in the landscape, such as that at Dundrum, had little power of obstruction in territorial defence, but that a territory could be well-protected by the coordination of castle locations within it. The regular spacing of Anglo-Norman *mottes*, especially on the north side of the River Liffey, constituted a protective cordon for the Anglo-Normans around the city of Dublin. It soon became clear that a similar strategy was needed on the south side to supplement the thirteenth-century castles built at Dundrum and Shankill.

TOWER HOUSES

During the fourteenth century, two further stone castles were built near streams to the south of Dublin – one at Carrickmines near the Ballyogan and Glenamuck Streams and the other at Shanganagh on the river of the same name. It would appear that at least the castle at Carrickmines was used from an early stage as a base for defence forces, as surviving accounts refer to troops of light horsemen and mounted archers being stationed there between 1360 and 1388. But by the fifteenth century, with the encouragement of the 1429 Subsidised Castles Act during the reign of Henry VI, a series of smaller castles or tower houses was built in the area stretching from Rathfarnham to Bray. Ultimately, some thirty of these fortified houses were built within Dún Laoghaire–Rathdown, in addition to the seven fortified store castles at Dalkey. The tower houses were not garrisoned castles like that at Carrickmines and, while some were larger than others, they normally had a walled enclosure or *bawn* attached where the owner's cattle could be protected in the event of a raid. Construction of the tower houses was subsidised because of the defence they offered to their owners but also for another reason. The tower houses helped to maintain large areas of land in Anglo-Norman or English control and it had become crucial that landowners should remain in possession of their lands against increasing attacks from the dispossessed Gaelic Irish, if the English colony around Dublin was to survive.

At that time, there was no concept of controlling access by way of a border or barrier and, contrary to what is sometimes believed, the tower houses of the fifteenth century did not form a line across Dún Laoghaire–Rathdown from Rathfarnham to Bray. These small castles were built on each major landholding and were dotted everywhere throughout the county between the River Dodder and the River Dargle.

KILGOBBIN CASTLE

The best surviving example in Dún Laoghaire–Rathdown of a typical tower house is Kilgobbin Castle, situated a short distance

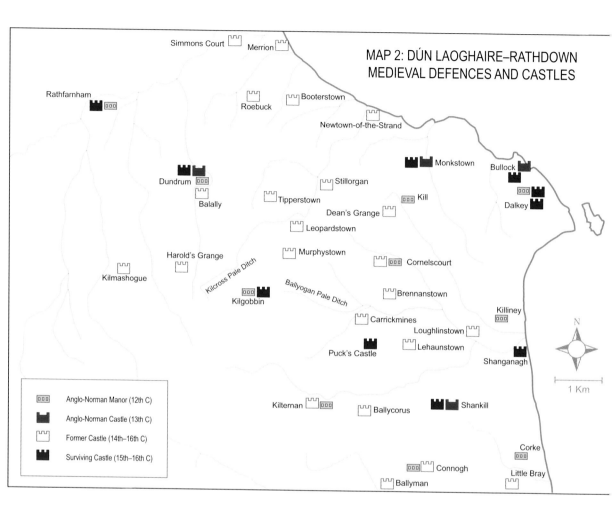

MAP 2: DÚN LAOGHAIRE–RATHDOWN MEDIEVAL DEFENCES AND CASTLES

Simmons Court · Merrion

Rathfarnham

Roebuck · Booterstown

Newtown-of-the-Strand

Monkstown · Bullock

Dundrum · Stillorgan · Dalkey

Balally · Tipperstown · Kill

Dean's Grange

Leopardstown

Harold's Grange · Murphystown

Kilmashogue · Kilcross Pale Ditch · Cornelscourt

Kilgobbin · Ballyogan Pale Ditch · Brennanstown

Killiney

Carrickmines

Loughlinstown

Puck's Castle · Lehaunstown

Shanganagh

N

1 Km

Anglo-Norman Manor (12th C)

Anglo-Norman Castle (13th C)

Former Castle (14th–16th C)

Surviving Castle (15th–16th C)

Kilternan · Ballycorus · Shankill

Corke

Connogh · Little Bray

Ballyman

from Stepaside village. It is located in private grounds on the left side of the road to Sandyford. Today it is an upright rectangular ruin, two storeys high over the ground floor, and it formerly had a thatched roof. Its thick walls of granite on the south and west sides rise to full height but the other two sides have fallen. The builders of Kilgobbin Castle were probably the Walsh family of Anglo-Norman descent, who were protecting their lands from the Harolds of Viking-Irish descent known for their continual

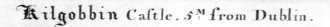

Fifteenth-century
tower house built
at Kilgobbin to
protect lands in
Anglo-Norman or
English control

burning and pillaging raids from the foothills of the Dublin Mountains.

Many other small defence castles, of which few traces remain today, are known to have existed in Dún Laoghaire–Rathdown at Ballyman, Balally, Ballycorus, Bray Little, Kilternan, Loughlinstown, Lehaunstown, Murphystown and Old Connaught.

However, significant traces remain to this day of larger

castles built not for defence purposes but to protect commercial interests. These were built by the Cistercian monks from the thirteenth century at Bullock Harbour to guard their fishing rights and on the Carrickbrennan Stream at Monkstown to protect their rich agricultural lands.

THE PALE

During the first half of the fifteenth century the area under the control of the Dublin administration declined in extent as more territory passed into the hands of so-called 'Irish enemies' and 'English rebels', the latter being rebellious descendents of the Anglo-Normans. The concept of a geographically-defined limitation of English authority in Ireland began to emerge and an official report in 1435 told Henry VI:

> …his land of Ireland is wellnigh destroyed, and inhabited
> with his enemies and rebels, so much so that there is not left
> in the nether parts of the counties of Dublin, Meath, Louth
> and Kildare, that join together, out of the subjection of the
> said enemies and rebels scarcely thirty miles in length and
> twenty miles in breadth there, as a man may surely ride or go
> in the said counties, to answer to the king's writs and to his
> commandments.

This English enclave became known as 'The Pale', a name derived from the Latin word *palus* meaning a stake and referring to the method of protective fencing using vertical stakes.

As the frontier of the Pale was a shifting one, it is not possible strictly to delineate its boundary but the lands within the Pale were entirely under the control of English settlers. Life here was stable, at both family and community level, mainly peaceful and with relatively little alteration in social balance. In contrast, the buffer zone which adjoined the Pale, known as the *marches*, was in a state of movement. Families of the Pale *marches* were expanding or contracting their estates in direct response to the pressures from the Gaelic Irish lordships beyond the *marches* in what was called the *maghery*. Some vigorously maintained their Englishness in language, customs and laws, while others became almost wholly Gaelic in law, custom and behaviour. Still others were both English and Irish, mixing cultural and legal prescriptions as suited their local family or personal interests or preferences. Both the Pale and the *marches* were to be found within Dún Laoghaire–Rathdown.

FRONTIER BOUNDARY

For most of the fifteenth century the frontier zone of the *inglishe pale* was manifest in the distribution of the defensive tower houses. By an act of parliament in 1488-9 the frontier was assigned a boundary, on paper rather than on the landscape. According to a medieval listing of the lands held by the Archbishop of Dublin, *Calendar of Archbishop Alen's Register*, the Pale extended in 1489 from Dalkey to the River Dodder protecting the lands of 'Dalkey, Monkstown, Newtown, Rochestown, Clonkeen, Smotscourt, Booterstown, Thorncastle and Blackrock.' A much later source, based on a note by the Rev G T Stokes published in the *Parish of Taney* by Francis E Ball and Everard Hamilton in 1895, described the extent of the Pale as follows:

> The Pale began at Dalkey and followed a south-westerly
> direction towards Kilternan; then turning northwards passed

View along
surviving Pale ditch
near the Ballyogan
Recycling Centre

Kilgobbin, where a castle still stands, and crossed the Parish of
Taney to the south of that part of the lands of Balally now called
Moreen, and thence in a westerly direction to Tallaght, and so
on to Naas in the Co of Kildare.

The frontier had no tangible boundaries in the cultural landscape
before 1494, but in that year an act of Poyning's parliament required
that the area defined as the Pale in 1488 was to be enclosed with
a 'double ditch of six feet high above ground on one side...which
mireth next unto Irishmen.' The 1494 act meant the construction
of a pair of ditches with a high bank between them, in order
to give some form of protection to the entire area rather than
merely to the landholdings protected by tower houses. The Pale

80

was not intended to be impassable but merely a hindrance to cattle-thieving raids by Gaelic Irish clans living in the '*magherys* beyond the Pale.' Earlier in the fifteenth century protective ditches, which were rural counterparts of town walls, had been erected but the Poyning's act of 1494 was a serious attempt to shore-up the contracting English colony within a single defensive entity. Despite the legal requirements, it is doubtful if this defence work was ever completed.

Part of Pale ditch as a landscape feature in Kilcross housing estate

DISCOVERY OF PALE DITCH

While local tradition has maintained that the Pale passed through certain areas of Dún Laoghaire–Rathdown, there had been no positive identification of this medieval defence until the mid-1970s. During the construction of the Kilcross housing estate local people alerted the builder to the significance of a raised feature on the land along the upper reaches of the Glaslower. This was subsequently examined by local archaeologist Patrick Healy and he found that the feature was a ditch about 220 metres long with a flat-topped bank flanked by two ditches. The bank was up to four metres wide at the top, six metres wide at the base and with ditches averaging about two metres wide. It was identified as portion of the medieval Pale ditch, and is today is preserved as a landscape feature in the middle of the Kilcross housing estate.

Subsequently, local historian Rob Goodbody identified another longer and better preserved portion of the Pale ditch at Ballyogan. This is in the form of a high flat-topped bank with large ditches on both sides. The bank is generally between two and three metres wide on top and stands up to two and a half metres above the present bottom of the ditches. The ditches vary from two metres to three metres wide. It appears that the depth of the ditches was originally greater, but gradual erosion of the bank has partly filled them in. There are hedgerow trees growing on the bank and some of them, particularly hawthorn, appear to be of great age. This ditch or earthwork stretches for a length of 500 metres, with three breaks through it: one is a farm lane; one is an access between fields and the third is where a sewer has been laid in the recent past. It is almost perfectly straight, except at its eastern end, where it curves slightly towards the nearby Ballyogan Stream. At the western end it meets the edge of the former Ballyogan tiphead and may originally have extended further westwards.

The position of this ditch would have been good for defensive purposes, as it lies at the edge of the flat floor of the valley which, even today, is damp and must have been fairly marshy in medieval times. This marshy area and the Ballyogan Stream lie to the south of the double ditch, which was the side facing the Gaelic Irish clans that the Pale was intended to keep out. As in the case of the other portion of the Pale discovered at Kilcross, strategic use was made of a watercourse, the Ballyogan Stream, to strengthen the Pale in medieval times.

CARRICKMINES CASTLE

In recent years, considerable controversy was caused when the site of the former castle at Carrickmines was threatened by the building of the extension of the M50 Motorway. A compromise was eventually reached whereby that portion of the site containing the more significant ruins would be preserved within the Carrickmines interchange.

This important castle was built near the confluence of the Ballyogan and Glenamuck streams in the fourteenth century as a fortified base for English defence forces. The first record of Carrickmines Castle refers to a troop of light horsemen being stationed there in 1360 under Sir John Bermingham. A large force under John Cottton, then Dean of St Patrick's and Treasurer of Ireland, afterwards Archbishop of Armagh, stayed there for periods during 1375 and there is also a record of forty mounted archers and light horsemen being based at Carrickmines in 1388.

During the fifteenth century, following the enactment of the Subsidised Castles Act 1429, a series of smaller castles or tower houses was built in the area stretching from Rathfarnham to Bray. These were fortified houses built on each major landholding and numbered some thirty in total. As they were positioned throughout the countryside, they helped to supplement the defence provided by the Carrickmines garrison. In 1441 Henry Walsh, of Anglo-Norman descent and described as 'Captain of the Walshmen', was associated with Carrickmines Castle and he is recorded as having been paid ten marks by the Crown for expenses 'in resisting the enemies of the King'. By the sixteenth century the Walsh family was in continuous occupation of the castle and were either tenants or owners of extensive lands stretching as far as Shanganagh, Old Connaught, Killegar, Kilgobbin, Balally, Killiney, Brennanstown and Leperstown. During the sixteenth and seventeenth centuries, the Walshes were one of the most important families in the area now known as Dún Laoghaire–Rathdown.

Records in the sixteenth century affirm that 'the Irish tribes were very troublesome' and that a troop of horse, numbering sixty men and known as the Earl of Southampton Horse, had to be based at Carrickmines. But they did not prove to be very useful as defenders for, according to the *Calendar of State Papers,* in the summer of 1599 the lands of Carrickmines were 'completely devastated by the Irish'. The Walsh family continued to occupy the castle and, in a report of 1630 on the diocese of Dublin, it is recorded that 'Mr Theobold Walsh maintained a priest and a friar to celebrate Mass and execute their functions in his mansion house at Carrickmines.'

1641 REBELLION

At the outbreak of the rebellion of 1641, families of Anglo-Norman descent were faced with a difficult choice. Alarmed at the success of the Puritans in the English Civil War, they were in great doubt whether or not they should side with an English government that distrusted them because they were Catholics and would not defend their property. Their alternative would be to join with the Gaelic Irish, who were their fellow Catholics. They chose the latter and in December 1641 allied themselves with the native Irish. Under the leadership of the Walshes, most of the county was soon in the hands of the rebels. On 12 February 1642, however, the rebels suffered a serious defeat at the battle of Deansgrange and fell back to Carrickmines Castle, which they had prepared for a siege.

Early in 1642 Charles I had agreed to send Sir Simon Harcourt to Ireland as Governor of Dublin and in a short time he had displayed extraordinary energy in gaining several victories against the rebels. On 26 March, Sir Simon decided to rid the area south of Dublin of rebels and headed for their stronghold at Carrickmines Castle. With '800 foot and as many horse as complete a troop of 250 men' he surrounded the castle and laid siege to it. When darkness fell, the defenders made a great fire on the roof of the castle, which was answered by one on the mountains. Fearing an ambush, Harcourt sent word to Dublin for more soldiers. Four hundred soldiers arrived by noon the next morning, with two great cannons. The besieging army now amounted to nearly 1500 men.

The castle defenders were not idle and used every opportunity to inflict losses on the besiegers by sorties and musket fire. They made a vigorous attempt to break through the cordon, but were driven back with heavy losses to the besiegers. At this time Harcourt with some of his officers had taken shelter behind a thatched cabin near the castle. For a moment, he rose up to instruct his soldiers but was spotted by a marksman in the castle who took deadly aim. Sir Simon Harcourt was shot with a bullet that pierced his right side under the neck. He was borne from the field and rushed to Lord Fitzwilliam's castle at Merrion, as he was too weak to bear the journey to Dublin. He did not survive and died the following day. He was buried in Christ Church Cathedral.

Lieutenant-Colonel Gibson then took command and vowed to seek revenge. He ordered a vigorous bombardment of the castle with the two cannons. Eventually a breach was made in the castle wall and the furious besiegers rushed in. Terrible and cruel slaughter followed and all who were within the castle – men, women and children numbering an estimated 300 people – were put to the sword. The castle was then blown up and the walls were levelled to the ground. Theobold Walsh, who apparently was not in the castle at the time of the siege, served afterwards as a captain in the Irish Confederate Army but did not return to Carrickmines.

After the Restoration of Charles II in 1660, Theobold Walsh's property was awarded to the Earl of Meath, who subsequently assigned it to Sir Joshua Allan of Stillorgan. But the story of the castle was at an end – that is until plans were prepared in the 1990s for extending the M50 Motorway over the remaining ruins of Carrickmines Castle.

The various medieval defences are shown on Map 2 (p 76), while Appendix III contains a list of the surviving castles and tower houses. Appendix IV lists the Martello towers built early in the nineteenth century to defend the coast from an anticipated French attack following the resumption of hostilities between England and Napoleonic France in 1803.

– 6 –

CROMWELL'S LEGACY

The Irish rebellion of 1641, the ensuing Eleven Years' War and the parallel Civil War in England had disastrous consequences for Ireland. Oliver Cromwell, the Puritan victor in the Civil War fought between King Charles I and Parliament, landed at Ringsend, south of Dublin, on 15 August 1649, motivated by religious and national bigotry. He was driven by the conviction that Irish Catholics shared collective blood-guilt for atrocities against Protestant settlers in 1641 and set out on a punitive campaign of destruction. In the words of a contemporary, Cromwell 'like lightening passed through the land'. The speed and decisiveness of his siege operations were remarkable and his brief nine-month campaign in Ireland added to his considerable reputation as a military leader. However, his desire for a punitive post-war settlement involving the forced transportation of many native Irish to Connaught under the slogan 'To Hell or to Connaught' earned Oliver Cromwell a niche in the demonology of Irish popular history.

THE *DOWN SURVEY*

The substantial task for the English government of apportioning several million acres of Irish land to soldiers who had been employed in suppressing the rebellious Irish since 1641 was organised through a unique operation known as the *Down Survey*.

The Parish of Mouncktowne
with its Boundes &c

The said Parish is bounded on the East wth the Sea ; on the South wth the Parish of Killeny ; on the West wth the parish of Kill ; & on the North wth the Parish of Doonabroocke.

Proprietors Name & his Qualificaçon	Denominaçon of Land	Number of Acres by by Estimate of yᵉ Countrey	Land profitable with its Quantity	Land unprofitable & Wast	Value of ye whole & each of ye said landes as was in 1640
Walter Cheevers of Mouncktowne Irish papist	Mouncktowne by Estimate foure plough-landes	foure hundred Thirty foure Acres	Acres : R : P Meadow 014 : 00 : 00 Arable 300 : 00 : 00 Rocky 120 : 00 : 00 pasture		By yᵉ Jury Two hundred poundes By us the same

OBSERVAÇONS

To yᵉ Proprietor	The Proprietor standes indicted for adhereing to the Rebells ; and possessed the said landes as his inheritance Anno. 1641.
To yᵉ Buildings	There is on the p'misses one old Castle newly repaired wth a Barne, Two garden plotts & an Orchard ; one Mill in use worth in 1640 Seaven poundes ; There is a small Creek for a haven the Jury value the Buildings at three hundred poundes being repaired by Lieutenant Generall Ludlow there is alsoe a parish Church in repaire
To yᵉ Woodes Mines &c	There is on the p'misses a Small shrubby wood, wth a few Ashtrees
To yᵉ Royaltyes & Tythes	The p'misses are a Mannor & kept Court Leet & Court Baron The Tythes did belong to the Proprietor
To yᵉ Boundes	The p'misses are Bounded on the East wth Bullock ; on the South wth Rochestowne ; on the West wth Stillorgan ; & on the North wth the Sea.

Fol. 12   **THE PARISH OF MOUNCKTOWNE**

Proprietors Name & his Qualificaçon	Denominaçon of Land	Number of Acres by Estimate of the Countrey	Land profitable & its Quantity	Land unprofitable & Wast	Value of ye whole & each of ye said landes as it was in 1640
Walter Cheevers of Mouncktowne Irish papist	Newtowne of stron by Estimate two ploughlandes	Two hundred and Twenty Acres	Acres : R : P Meadow 001 : 00 : 00 Arable 120 : 00 : 00 Rocky Pasture } 100 : 00 : 00		By ye Jury Eighty poundes By us the same

The physician-general to the army in Ireland, Sir William Petty, had gained a reputation for effective administration and he was given the task of measuring and mapping the estates that were to be confiscated under the Cromwellian land settlement. Unlike the preliminary *Civil Survey*, expressed in verbal and numerical form, the information Petty collected was marked down on maps, thus giving rise to the name *Down Survey*. The success of Petty's system not only allowed land settlements to be effected with remarkable efficiency; his surveys influenced mapping methods throughout Ireland for more than a century and provided the basis for the first atlas of Ireland published in 1685. As may be seen from the map on page 90, the details recorded in both the *Civil* and *Down* surveys from 1654 to 1656 provide, immediately following the Cromwellian conquest, a most valuable legacy and insight to the state of the area we now know as Dún Laoghaire–Rathdown.

THE *CIVIL SURVEY*

Towards the end of the seventeenth century the first map of County Dublin was published by William Petty. It is most interesting as it shows the eleven medieval parishes that constituted at that time the Halfe-Barony of Rathdowne, roughly equivalent to the County of Dún Laoghaire–Rathdown today. This area was described as follows in the *Civil Survey* in 1655:

> The said halfe Barony is bounded on the East wth the Sea; on the south wth Brey; on the West wth Rathfarnam in the Barony of New Castle; & on the North wth the Rings-end.

Extract from
1655 *Civil Survey*
showing part of
Monkstown parish

89

90

It is in length Eight miles; & in Breadth foure Miles; that is to say from the river of Doonabrook to the river of Brey Eight Miles.

The Soyle thereof for the most part is dry & hott, having noe Woods, Boggs, Mines, or Quarryes thereon, onely some rocky pastures wch are beneficiall.

The said halfe Barony containes Eleaven parishes whose names are

Donabrooke	Tully
Tannee	White Church
Kill	Kilternan
Munkstowne	Kilgobban
Killenye	Rath Michell

Connagh

From the reproduced copy of Petty's map, it will be noted that the former major Early Christian centres of Balally, Kilternan, Tully and Kill, together with Rathfarnam, are shown prominently, signifying their continued importance when the map was drawn about 1685. As well as the inland medieval manorial centres and castles already referred to, eighteen further castles are shown at 'Simmons Court, Merrion, Butterstowne, Newtowne of the Strand, Monkstowne, Bullock, Dauky, Robuck, Tiberstowne, Moltanstowne, Stillorgan, Deans Grange, Cornellscourt, Leperds-towne, Loghanstowne, Loghcastowne, Connogh and Little Bray'. Three further castles are referred to in the 1655 *Civil Survey*, at Brennanstown, Kilmashogue and Harold's Grange. It is of interest that many of the additional castles had been built along the Shanganagh River system, indicating the importance of that watercourse in defence.

Extract from William Petty's 1685 map, *The County of Dublin*

MONKSTOWN CASTLE

The castle at Monkstown has an interesting history, and it featured in Oliver Cromwell's infamous scheme to transport all the native Irish to Connaught. When Henry II came to Dublin in 1172 following the Anglo-Norman invasion he decreed that large areas of land in Dún Laoghaire–Rathdown should be retained by the archbishop and monasteries of Dublin. Prior to the invasion, the Cistercian monks of St Mary's Abbey had held all the lands stretching from Bullock Harbour through Glenageary and Sallynoggin to Monkstown, including the creek at Dunleary where the Strad Brook and Carrickbrennan Streams entered the sea. Early in the thirteenth century the monks built a castle beside the Carrickbrennan Stream and close to an Early Christian church of the same name. They developed the surrounding fertile lands, established a grange and engaged in farming for over 300 years in an extensive area, part of which is still known as Monkstown Farm.

Following the Reformation and the dissolution of the monasteries by Henry VIII in 1539, the monks were dispossessed of their property and their rich lands were granted to Sir Arthur Travers, a man highly regarded by the king. Travers was made Master of the Ordinance in Ireland and was one of the chief military adventurers of the sixteenth century, who had the advantage of being able to speak Irish. After Travers the castle and lands passed to the Cheevers family, who held it until they were dispossessed after the Cromwellian conquest, because of 'adhereing to the Rebells.' On 19 December 1653, Walter Cheevers, his family and many retainers were transported to Connaught in compliance with Cromwell's direction 'To Hell or to Connaught'.

After the resettlement, Monkstown Castle and its lands were given to General Edmund Ludlow, a colleague and follower of

Monckstown . 2.d View .

Oliver Cromwell and one of the signatories of the death warrant of Charles I. He was appointed as Commander of the Horse in Ireland and, although a staunch supporter of Cromwell when he arrived in August 1649, he later became disillusioned with Cromwell's tactics in Ireland. When Henry Cromwell, son of Oliver, arrived in June 1654, Ludlow entertained him at Monkstown Castle, showed him the pleasure grounds and gardens he was developing but expressed concern at his father's violent government. He told Henry bluntly that he totally disapproved of Oliver Cromwell's adoption of the

Gardens at Monkstown Castle, as shown in an eighteenth-century painting

title Lord Protector. After Cromwell's death, General Ludlow became commander-in-chief of the army in Ireland. However in 1660, after the Restoration of Charles II, Monkstown Castle was returned to the Cheevers family and Ludlow found himself at the top of the list for execution because of his anti-royalist views. He escaped to Switzerland, where he lived in exile under constant threat of assassination attempts until his death in 1692.

The antiquary Austin Cooper, writing in 1780, described Monkstown Castle as comprising 'two square towers, a ninety-foot tower and a house in the Gothic style, three storeys high, with saloon, library, gallery and chapel – the second finest house in south Co Dublin.' A magnificent garden comprised icehouses, greenhouses and furnaces. Today all that remains are a gate-tower and the shell of the house. The gardens were taken over for building development and among the modern houses may be found a few desolate yew trees that once formed a stately walk.

PROTO-INDUSTRIES

After the great land transfers from Catholic to Protestant owner-ship following the Cromwellian conquest, the manorial system was replaced by a more modern commercial landlord-tenant relationship. In the Dún Laoghaire–Rathdown area, however, many of the Old Catholic landlords of Anglo-Norman descent managed to hold on to their estates and their lands were not fragmented, as happened in many other parts of the country. This was of great importance to future development as it helped to ensure that the small centres of population that had already developed were kept intact and further expanded. Locations suitable for proto-, or early, industrial development were first to benefit from the relative stability of the county in the late seventeenth and early eighteenth

centuries. Many of the small concentrations of population were
along rivers and streams and they began to exploit waterpower
to develop proto-industries. For example, a medieval mill at
Kilgobbin was developed, perhaps as a corn mill for the castle.
However, the water supply at Kilgobbin on the upper reaches of
the Ballyogan Stream would not have been consistent throughout
the year. A mill there could not compete against other mills with
a constant water supply that enabled them to operate without
restriction and grow into large concerns. Therefore, the larger
mills that developed in the eighteenth century were established
lower down the streams and rivers: at Kilternan, Shanganagh,
Dundrum and Rathfarnham. It was around these larger mills that
people began to settle as early as the eighteenth century. A map
of the Fitzwilliam Estate at Dundrum in 1762 and a map of the
Roberts Estate at Shanganagh in 1826 show that small settlements
of houses were already forming at these mill locations.

MARLAY PARK

Another development in the eighteenth century that could have
contributed to further centres of population in Dún Laoghaire–
Rathdown was the creation of a number of large demesnes. One
of the largest demesnes to remain intact in the county to this day
is the 400-acre Marlay Park. All the original trees and planting
survive intact and much of the original estate wall is also in place.
The house, with its large stableyard and farmyards some way off,
is also a perfect example of an eighteenth-century estate. Marlay
Park is located on the Little Dargle River, where an artificial
lake and a small island were constructed as part of improvements
made by the eighteenth-century banker David La Touche, when
he purchased the property, then known as The Grange, from

THE STILLORGAN OBELISK

♦ At the top of Carysfort Avenue on the right-hand side if one is coming up from Blackrock is one of the finest obelisks of its kind in Ireland. It was built in 1727 by Lord Allen of Stillorgan Park during one of the eighteenth-century famines, principally to provide employment in the area but also as a monument to Lady Allen who was to have been buried there. The tall granite obelisk, some seventeen metres high, is perched on a cross-vaulted, rock-covered base, and steep steps enable the visitor to climb up and enter a small domed chamber at the bottom of the obelisk and admire the view. The obelisk was designed by Edward Lovett Pearce, who also designed the Irish Houses of Parliament building, now Bank of Ireland, on College Green, Dublin. Pearce spent much of his time in Rome and would have been inspired by a very similar obelisk by Giovanni Bernini in the Piazza Navona.

It is of interest that Lord Allen, to whose ancestors were assigned all the lands expropriated from Theobold Walsh of Carrickmines Castle following the 1641 rebellion, was himself the subject of a satire by Dean Swift who described him perhaps harshly:

> Positive and overbearing
> Changing still and still adhering,
> Spiteful, peevish, rude, untoward,
> Fierce in tongue, in heart a coward,
> Reputation ever tearing,
> Ever dearest friendship swearing,
> Judgement weak and passion strong,
> Always various, always wrong.

Lady Allen died in 1758 and was buried in London, where she moved after her husband's death, and not as intended beneath the Stillorgan Park Obelisk. But in 1955 a remarkable discovery was made at the base of the obelisk of another much older burial of a woman. A Bronze Age *cist* burial was found containing the disturbed remains of the skeleton of an adult female, whose death seemed to have been caused by a sacrificial blow to the skull. ♦

1727 Stillorgan
Park Obelisk
as a feature in
Carysfort Woods
housing estate

Thomas Taylor, Lord Mayor of Dublin, in 1764. La Touche married Elizabeth Marlay, daughter of the Bishop of Dromore, and renamed the house after her. He laid out the demesne, built a threshing mill on the Little Dargle River and created Marlay House in its present form with its elegant rooms. A magnificent new ballroom facing the Dublin Mountains, an oval music room and an elegant staircase were added to the house. All the rooms contain decorative plasterwork of high quality. Now owned by Dún Laoghaire–Rathdown County Council, Marlay House is open for public viewing.

STILLORGAN PARK

Another large demesne, Stillorgan Park, was created in the eighteenth century when fish ponds and decorative lakes were developed along the Glaslower near the site of the former medieval manor of Stillorgan. An imposing new house was built in 1695 for Lord Allen, Earl of Carysfort, who had benefited from the resettlement of the Walsh lands at Carrickmines following the Cromwellian conquest. During the eighteenth century the family became prominent in public life and Sir Joshua Allen became Lord Mayor of Dublin. Local historian, Peter Pearson, believes that, had Stillorgan Park House remained intact with its magnificent demesne, there is little doubt that it would be one of the largest and most important historic properties in the county. The Allen estate stretched from Stillorgan village across to Newtownpark Avenue, down to Blackrock, and up Mount Merrion Avenue. It covered all of what now are Priory Park, Grove Avenue, Avoca Avenue, Stillorgan Grove and Carysfort Avenue. Stillorgan Park House faced north towards Mount Merrion Avenue and stood at the head of a long grove of trees planted three rows deep on either side.

The magnificent grounds contained a tall granite obelisk, formal avenues, various carriage drives and three rectangular fishponds, which were located below the present St John of God Hospital in Stillorgan. Early in the twentieth century, the Stillorgan Park Golf Club existed on part of these lands but closed after only nine years in 1917. It was the golf club that filled in the artificial lakes on the Glaslower.

CABINTEELY PARK

A third large demesne in Dún Laoghaire–Rathdown was Cabinteely Park, created in the eighteenth century around the former medieval manor of Cornelscourt located on St Bride's Stream. The lands originally belonged to the Byrne family, the ruin of whose medieval castle had been surrounded by cottages and marked on the earliest ordnance survey map published in 1837. Cabinteely House and demesne are situated on high ground from which extensive views may be had of Killiney, Rochestown and Sallynoggin. The house was built in 1769 by Lord Clare, who was related by marriage to the Byrnes but the original building's external appearance was substantially altered in the nineteenth century. However, the original doorcase remains, together with the roofline urns and two beautiful rooms. The drawing room on the first floor has a coved ceiling which is delicately ornamented with classical plasterwork plaques, cornices and friezes. The eighteenth-century staircase, also decorated with plasterwork, leads to a long vaulted gallery and ten bedrooms. In the hall is a fine eighteenth-century sandstone chimneypiece which features busts and musical instruments. For most of the nineteenth century the Byrnes lived at Cabinteely but the house and lands were sold in 1933 to the McGrath family, who presented the house and part of the land to Dublin County Council in 1969. Eight years later, 200 acres of the former demesne were sold for private housing development. Now owned by Dún Laoghaire–Rathdown County Council, Cabinteely House is open for public viewing.

− 7 −

Industries on Rivers and Streams

The relative stability of Dún Laoghaire–Rathdown in the late seventeenth and early eighteenth centuries encouraged landowners to improve their estates and consider new developments that could enhance their property and prosperity. They began to examine the potential of rivers and streams flowing through their properties and many successfully developed proto-industries by this means. Small mills based on rivers and streams had been a central feature of early Irish society and, in the manorial economy of the medieval period, the lord of the manor usually provided a water mill to grind corn for his tenants. Such a central facility in each manor often encouraged people to settle nearby and in time the mills became an essential component of early population settlements.

Harnessing Water Power

In the nineteenth century, as water mills developed, they were often combined with other early industrial activity and led to the creation of new settlements. An examination of early maps reveals that most industrial activity developed beside the fast-flowing waters around Rockbrook on the Owendoher River and Whitechurch Stream, around Dundrum on the River Slang, and at Kilternan on the Loughlinstown River. With increasing technical knowledge during the century, water power was harnessed for much wider manufacturing and service purposes than mere corn grinding. For example, around Rockbrook paper mills, cloth mills and a cotton mill developed, all powered by the Owendoher River. The first ordnance survey map of the area in 1840 showed no fewer than ten mills along the Owendoher River between Rockbrook and Ballyboden. At Whitechurch, cloth mills and a laundry mill operated on the waterpower of the Whitechurch Stream, while within the Marlay Park demesne a threshing mill was powered by the Little Dargle River. Map 3 (p 104) shows the extent of industrial activity in Dún Laoghaire–Rathdown at this time.

On the lower reaches of these rivers, where they joined the River Dodder at Rathfarnham, there were many larger water-powered industries providing considerable employment in a wide area of the county during the nineteenth and early twentieth centuries. Landy's Millrace, which is now gone, ran from Willbrook through Rathfarnham Castle grounds, feeding the ornamental lake and serving Landy's Bakery in Rathfarnham village. It then passed through a sawmill before joining the River Dodder. According to local historian Christopher Ryan, Rathfarnham formerly accommodated four mills – a flourmill, a corn mill and two paper mills. Around Dundrum on the River Slang, there was a paper mill, as well as three millwheels and an ironworks. Downriver from Dundrum, at Farrenboley near the old village of Windy Arbour, a flour mill and a sawmill operated as well as a paper mill served by a large millpond. The considerable employment provided by these water-powered industries in the nineteenth century certainly contributed to the growth of sizeable settlements around Rathfarnham and Dundrum.

BREWING, MILLING AND MINING

Uniquely, on the Glaslower at Stillorgan a brewery operated for over a century. Located near the junction of Brewery Road and the N11 Dublin–Bray road, it was described by Samuel Lewis in the 1837 *Topographical Dictionary of Ireland* as:

> Close to the village is an ale and beer brewery, which has
> carried on for more than 80 years by the family of Darley. It
> has been for more than 40 years in the possession of the present
> propriety, who have also an extensive brewery and malting
> concern at Bray.

A surviving plan of Darley's Brewery shows the diversion of the Glaslower through the centre of the plant, indicating the importance of water to this industry in Stillorgan in the nineteenth century.

In the south of Dún Laoghaire–Rathdown other industrial plants were developed on both the Loughlinstown and Shanganagh Rivers. At Kilternan on the Loughlinstown River a paper mill and a cotton mill developed in the eighteenth century; each employed forty people in 1837. Further down the same river, at Ballycorus, the Mining Company of Ireland developed lead-processing works at the beginning of the nineteenth century. On the Shanganagh River at Loughlinstown there were two corn mills and a tuck mill. In addition to these industries developed in the eighteenth and nineteenth centuries on the various rivers and streams, there were small private water mills at Kilgobbin on the Ballyogan Stream and at Kill-of-the-Grange on the Dean's Grange Stream.

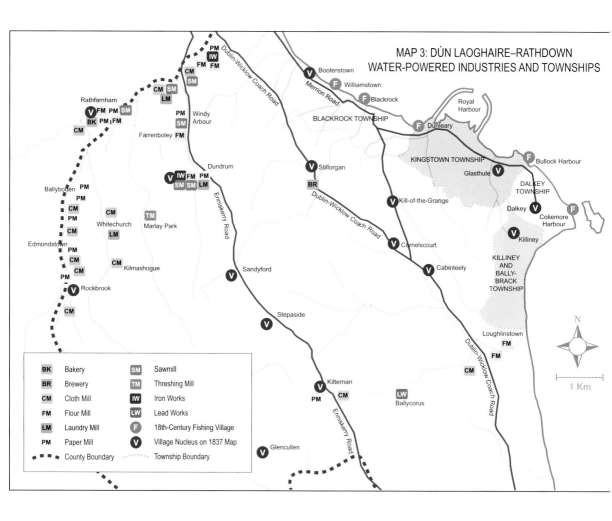

MAP 3: DÚN LAOGHAIRE–RATHDOWN
WATER-POWERED INDUSTRIES AND TOWNSHIPS

BK	Bakery	SM	Sawmill
BR	Brewery	TM	Threshing Mill
CM	Cloth Mill	IW	Iron Works
FM	Flour Mill	LW	Lead Works
LM	Laundry Mill	F	18th-Century Fishing Village
PM	Paper Mill	V	Village Nucleus on 1837 Map
▪▪▪	County Boundary	⋯⋯	Township Boundary

WATER MILLS

Since the earliest recorded history in Ireland water mills have
been regarded as important and valuable. In the Old Irish law
texts of the seventh century there may be found *Coibnes Uisci
Thairidne*, (kinship of conducted water), which laid down the
rules for conducting water across a neighbour's land to power a
mill. Another related law text is *Bechbretha* (bee-judgements),

which deals with trespass by bees, bee-stings and the ownership of swarms. Clearly, early Irish society laid great importance on protecting water and bees, both being key to greater wealth and health.

In the manorial system of land management introduced by the Anglo-Normans, a water mill was a central feature of the manor, enabling the lord to provide corn milling for his tenants. Following the Cromwellian conquest, the *Civil Survey* conducted from 1654 to 1656 reveals that water mills were adjuncts to most of the major houses and castles in Dún Laoghaire–Rathdown, and, when relatively stable conditions prevailed in the late seventeenth and early eighteenth centuries, major landowners concentrated on exploiting the potential of water mills to develop new manufacturing and services.

By scanning old maps – such as William Duncan's map of 1821 or the 1837 copperplate first edition of the ordnance survey – we can discover the sites of many old mills along the rivers and streams of Dún Laoghaire–Rathdown. Even though the old mill buildings may no longer exist, a visit to the site could lead to the discovery of a weir, a millpond or perhaps an empty millrace. While the original mill at many sites may only have been grinding corn, by the eighteenth century the waters were often turning wheels for manufacturing woollen cloth, printing cotton, making paper or sawing wood.

The earliest mills were worked directly off a stream, without the help of weir, millpond or millrace. Production was at the mercy of the weather. If it was too dry, there was no power and, with heavy winter rain, a stream in spate could make milling too dangerous. An early development was to slice a bit off the stream, build a millrace and control the flow of water to the mill by sluices. A millpond guaranteed water supply in dry weather and the combination of a millpond, millrace and sluices allowed the miller to control water levels and maintain constant levels of production. The function of the weir was to direct some of the water from the river or stream into the millrace and millpond. It acted as a dam in dry weather and, when the river was swollen in flood, all the excess water flowed off over the top of the weir.

Although most water mills have now passed into history, water power to this day still turns three turbines at the preserved Shackleton's Mill on the River Liffey at Lucan, as well as the great turbines of the two hydro-electric power stations nearest Dún Laoghaire–Rathdown, at Poulaphuca and at Leixlip on the River Liffey.

DECLINE OF WATER POWER

Following the Act of Union in 1801, circumstances and legislation conspired to undermine Irish industry generally and many of the early industries were unable to withstand the competition of larger English concerns. The early nineteenth century saw a relative decline in traditional non-agricultural activity and increased regional concentration in industries such as textiles and paper-making. These small industries that developed beside the fast-flowing rivers around Rockbrook survived for too short a time to have any lasting impact on the settlement pattern. The paper and cotton mills at Kilternan had an impact on settlement for a while, but when their viability was eroded by competition from larger plants they were obliged to close. The *Statistical Survey of County Dublin 1801* stated that paper manufacturing appeared to be declining and that several mills had stopped working and were going to ruin. Some industrial plants, however, were more robust and they had an influence on their surroundings. The water-powered industries at Rathfarnham on the River Dodder

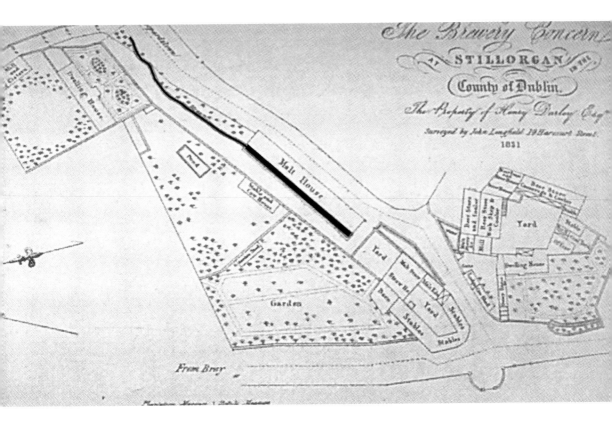

and at Dundrum on the River Slang continued to prosper and they contributed to the growth of these villages well into the twentieth century.

 With the development of steam and, especially, electricity as forms of power in the first half of the twentieth century, the use of water for industrial power declined. Rivers and streams became less critical in choosing potential sites for new industries and gradually the concentration of industrial activity along the watercourses of Dún Laoghaire–Rathdown diminished. Mills and plants along the Owendoher River and Whitechurch Stream closed, as more efficient production units could be sited closer to Dublin powered by the new national electricity grid from

1831 plan of Darley's Brewery showing the Glaslower running through

BALLYCORUS LEAD WORKS

♦ As one travels south towards Bray on the N11 beyond Cabinteely an old chimney is visible on top of a distant hill on the right-hand side of the road. It marks the location of extensive lead works that were developed beside the Loughlinstown River in the nineteenth century.

The Mining Company of Ireland began activities here about 1807, shortly after lead ore was discovered, and by 1824 two veins of lead were being worked. Silver was also once found here in considerable quantities. The landmark granite chimney with its external spiral staircase on Ballycorus Hill was for many years shown on admiralty charts as a point of reference for mariners. The chimney and its lengthy flue, which ran for two kilometres, carried the highly poisonous fumes away from the works in the river valley where the lead was being processed. The flue is of stone construction with a brick roof and was sealed with a layer of earth. Substantial parts of the flue with its inspecting doors still exist and can be explored.

In the nineteenth century an extensive settlement was built by the company above the Loughlinstown River at Ballycorus, comprising a manager's house in granite, workers' cottages also in granite, a water pond, water wheel, furnaces, purification tanks, lime kilns and various stores. A shot tower, where shot or bullets were manufactured, was also built and has survived. It has been restored along with some other old buildings. Shot was made by pouring molten lead from a height, through a perforated tool, into water far below where it cooled into a perfect ball. The lead works remained in operation until early in the twentieth century, providing lead piping for Dublin's new Vartry water supply system and also lead roof-sheeting for housing in Dublin.

When the business collapsed at the outbreak of the First World War, the extensive plant was closed and the settlement subsequently dispersed. Some light industry is still located at the site of the old lead works but almost all of the housing is now abandoned. When the lead deposits at Ballycorus became exhausted in the nineteenth century, most of the lead ore was transported from Glendasan in County Wicklow by horse and cart to Rathdrum, thence by rail to Shankill Station on the old Harcourt Street line, from where it was again carted to the smelting works at Ballycorus. ♦

Nineteenth-century chimney
with external spiral staircase
on Ballycorus Hill

1930 onwards. Those in the southern part of the county along the Loughlinstown and Shanganagh Rivers had already closed by the end of the nineteenth century, as had the brewery on the Glaslower at Stillorgan. The last mill at Dundrum, on the site of the Anglo-Norman manor, was transformed in 1876 into a laundry but retained its historic name, becoming the Manor Mill Laundry. It continued to employ considerable numbers in the area for over half a century. In 1943 it was taken over by Pye Ireland Ltd as a facility for the manufacture of cabinets for radio and television sets, and continued to provide much employment in Dundrum until technological change forced its closure in 1985. The site has now been absorbed into the large modern complex known as Dundrum Town Centre.

VILLAGE GROWTH

Close examination of the first ordnance survey maps produced from 1837 onwards reveals that small nucleated settlements grew in Dún Laoghaire–Rathdown during the eighteenth and nineteenth centuries. A nucleated settlement, or village, was defined as having a church building as a minimal indicator of a meeting-place function. Many of these settlements were along the new main coach roads inland from Dublin to Bray and to Enniskerry, while other new villages grew following the patterns of earlier sites established along rivers and streams. For example, on the Owendoher River a small industrial village had developed at Rockbrook and another larger village grew at Rathfarnham near the sites of an Early Christian church and the medieval manor.

On the coach road from Dublin to Enniskerry, a further large village developed at Dundrum on the River Slang with industrial mills in the valley below the Anglo-Norman castle and the site

of the medieval manor. Further along the road, at Sandyford on
the Glaslower, a chapel village grew, with just a church and some
houses, while at Kilternan, another site of an Early Christian church
and medieval manor, a village had formed near the industrial mills
developed on the Loughlinstown River.

On the coach road to Bray, a village had grown at Stillorgan
near the confluence of the Kilmacud Stream and the Glaslower,
just below the site of an Early Christian church, the medieval
manor and the new brewery. At Cornelscourt, the site of another
medieval manor, a small village had formed on St Bride's Stream
and, a short distance beyond at Cabinteely, a small chapel village
had been established. On the road from Blackrock to Cabinteely,
a village had also emerged at Kill-of-the-Grange on the Dean's

Grange Stream, near the site of an Early Christian church.

Along the coastal road to Dalkey, apart from the old-established fishing villages of Blackrock, Dunleary and Dalkey, new villages had appeared at Booterstown, Williamstown, and Glasthule, the latter on a stream of the same name. Other villages marked on the first 1837 ordnance survey maps included Stepaside, near the Early Christian and Anglo-Norman site of Kilgobbin, Killiney located on a hillside near the old lead mine workings and Glencullen on a river of the same name, with just a chapel and some houses.

– 8 –

KINGSTOWN AND OTHER TOWNSHIPS

John Roque's map of 1757 shows two fishing villages on the southern shore of Dublin Bay at the mouths of small rivers or streams. Near the mouth of the Glaslower is shown Black Rocktown and beyond the confluence of the Strad Brook and Rochestown Stream is shown Dunleary at the head of a small creek. Both of these small settlements were long-established fishing villages and Dunleary was also the location of a noted salt works on the seaward side of a hill known as Salthill. In the eighteenth century Dunleary was a compact and complete village of seventy dwellings or cottages. Some fifteen houses, including the present Purty Kitchen, comprised a row of dwellings which is all that remains of the original village.

VILLAS NEAR THE SEA

In the eighteenth century it became the fashion among the gentry to build large houses or villas as their residences on the periphery of the city. The first large houses were built on higher ground with sea views and two large estates with fine views over Dublin Bay were established at Mount Merrion by Lord Fitzwilliam and at Stillorgan by the Allen family. Great changes followed and, by the beginning of the nineteenth century, new villas were being built closer to the coast and in many cases on sites overlooking the sea.

A study of William Duncan's map of 1821 shows that Blackrock became dotted with many houses, gardens and well-planted small estates. Many of the new houses were built along the course of the Priory Stream, the Glaslower and the Strad Brook, resulting in clusters of villas being developed in the area now extending from Blackrock through Monkstown to Dún Laoghaire. Even today, parts of Blackrock and Monkstown have the air of exclusively residential areas with a definite character and architectural style. The number of villas in early Victorian or sometimes Regency styles, and the abundance of trees, hedges and gardens, along with many stone walls and the variety of architecture, make Blackrock and Monkstown most appealing residential areas.

From *Thom's Directory* it is possible to build up a picture of the extent of suburban expansion around Dublin. Ribbon development along the main arteries from the city was the usual pattern, with individual villa-type houses springing up, succeeded in time by semi-detached and terraced dwellings. Roads were built off the main thoroughfares to open up new land for housing, and many of these roads eventually became link roads between the main arteries. A process of infilling then began in areas already possessing small scattered villages. *Thom's Directory* of 1853 provides a record that the village of Booterstown had a population of 535 living in 109 houses and shows that ribbon development had taken place to such an extent that it was said to be almost continuous with Williamstown to the south and Merrion to the north. Blackrock had a population of nearly 2500 and was described as consisting of one main and several minor streets and avenues containing 485 houses 'well but irregularly built'. Blackrock was stated to be standing 'in a diversified country, studded with numerous marine and other pleasing villas, embellished with tastefully laid out grounds, commanding fine views of the sea and mountains.' Dunleary had been a mere fishing village before the building of the new harbour but had grown to a population of some 10,500 by 1853. Dalkey was described as a picturesque village at the extremity of Dublin Bay 'eight miles from the General Post Office in Sackville Street'. It had forty houses and a population of 250. Killiney, to the south of Dalkey, was so undeveloped that it did not merit inclusion in *Thom's Directory* at that time.

SEA TRAGEDIES

A distressing feature of the early years of the nineteenth century was the frequency of shipwrecks and sea tragedies that afflicted the rocky southern coast of Dublin Bay.

A double sea tragedy occurred in a heavy snowstorm driven by a violent easterly gale in 1807, when some 385 people were dashed to death on the sharp and irregular rocks of the coast between Blackrock and Dún Laoghaire. Two sailing troopships, the *Prince of Wales* and the *Rochdale,* carrying volunteers for foreign service drawn from Irish militia regiments that were used to quell the 1798 and 1803 rebellions, left Pigeon House Harbour, Dublin, on the afternoon of 18 November 1807. The morning after their departure, both ships were observed labouring in heavy seas outside Dublin Bay trying to return to the harbour, but as the day advanced heavy snow began to fall, severely limiting visibility. The sea then became so rough in a rising easterly gale that it was not even possible for the ships to anchor. After a long and futile struggle, by nightfall the ships were being driven inexorably towards the rocky shores south of Blackrock.

In the darkness of the night the captain of the *Prince of Wales* launched a longboat and, together with some crew and soldiers, he managed to row along the coast into shallow water near Maretimo and make his way to Blackrock. For some extraordinary reason, no

115

effort seems to have been made that night to rescue the remaining passengers on board and by daybreak some 120 of those left to their fate on the stricken ship had perished. All were buried in the old graveyard at Merrion near the Tara Towers Hotel.

An even worse fate befell the *Rochdale*. Although several anchors were thrown, the ship was driven gradually by the gale towards the shore at Sandycove. In total darkness and blinding snow, the ship was swept past the old pier at Dunleary and driven onto the rocks beneath the Martello Tower at Seapoint, just a short

distance south of where the *Prince of Wales* had struck the jagged coast at Maretimo. The nineteenth-century writer Weston St John Joyce described the final hours of the unfortunates on board:

Embarkation of King George IV from Kingstown Harbour on 3 September 1821

> When the ill-fated vessel was being driven past the old pier at
> Dunleary, inhabitants of adjoining houses could hear the cries
> of the terrified passengers and the reports of the muskets they
> were firing to attract assistance. Some people on the east side
> of the old harbour seeing the flashes and hearing the reports,

ran around to the westward in the hope of affording help, but
on reaching the road at Salthill they were obliged to lie down
behind the parapet abutting on the sea to protect themselves
from the bullets being fired in the dark by the despairing troops
on board.

Of the troops on board, their families, the ship's officers and crew,
not a single soul escaped and some 265 perished in all. Their
mutilated bodies were found in great numbers over the following
days strewn along the shore. According to Joyce, the wrecked
vessel was poised in an extraordinary manner on the rocks at the
front of the Martello Tower and lay so close to the shore that a
twelve-foot plank sufficed to reach her quarter-deck. But at the
time she struck the night was so dark and the snowstorm so dense
that the unhappy passengers were doubtless unable to see anything
off the vessel and, consequently, were unaware of their proximity
to the land. Nearly 400 lives were lost in this double disaster. For
days afterwards the bodies of men, women and children were cast
up by the sea along the coast from Merrion to Dunleary.

The bodies of the *Rochdale* victims were in almost every
case unrecognisable owing to the manner in which they were
dashed to death on the rocks or torn to pieces by the action of the
sea in the hold of the vessel after she began to break up. Most of
these victims were interred in the old Carickbrennan churchyard,
opposite Monkstown Castle.

NEW ROYAL HARBOUR

The danger to sailing ships of the approaches to the mouth of the
River Liffey and the double sea tragedies of November 1807 led
to a strong campaign for the building of 'an asylum harbour for the

YACHTING AT KINGSTOWN

♦ Yachting was established as a sport in Dublin Bay during the early nineteenth century and the New Royal Harbour at Kingstown with its broad expanse of water was ideal for this fashionable new sport. Unlike Howth or Bullock at that time, the harbour never dried out at low water. The Royal Irish Yacht Club was founded in 1831 and built an elegant clubhouse in a central position in the harbour. Another clubhouse was completed in neo-classical style in 1843 for the Royal St George Yacht Club and finally in 1870 a further yacht club, the National Yacht Club, established its premises on the harbour front. These clubs quickly assembled a prestigious and elite membership from the titled, professional and landed classes.

In the middle of the nineteenth century, yachts tended to be very large and required considerable funds for their operation and crewing. It was only later in the century that smaller and more affordable boats were developed. Kingstown can claim to have developed the first one-design dinghy in the world, a small racing yacht of identical design to the rest of its fleet. It is still called the *Water Wag*, looks like a rowing boat with sails and was first built in 1878.

Lavish regattas became a seasonal event at Kingstown, with bigger and bigger yachts arriving in the harbour each year. Ships would be decked out in bunting, military bands played on the East Pier and spectacular firework displays were held at night. In 1869, James J Gaskin painted this scene of elegance, wealth and privilege:

> At the Royal yacht clubs the *crème de la crème* of the aristocracy and gentry assemble during the Kingstown regatta, which generally takes place in August. The usual gaiety of the place during this aquatic carnival is much increased by the appearance of the harbour, which contains an immense assemblage of elegant pleasure vessels of every size and rig, from the ship and steamer of 500 tons burthen to the yawl of only ten.

While all was well for the privileged, their lifestyle contrasted sharply with the poverty and deprivation witnessed by Charles Halliday in 1844 when he was campaigning to rid Kingstown of its many overcrowded hovels that had no proper water supply or sanitation. ♦

port of Dublin' nearer the mouth of Dublin Bay. After much debate about the best location, particularly in the light of the unsuccessful operation of Howth Harbour, it was decided to construct two long granite piers at Dunleary that would embrace some 250 acres of water and provide shelter to ships even in the severest weather conditions. This major development in the early part of the nineteenth century accounted for a huge growth in the population of Dún Laoghaire–Rathdown. Work was begun in 1815 and took over forty years to complete at a cost of one million pounds – a huge sum in mid-nineteenth century Ireland. The foundation stone of the New Royal Harbour was laid in 1817 by the English lord lieutenant and the subsequent visit by George IV to Dunleary in 1821 greatly enhanced this prestigious project. Most notably, it led to the formal adoption of the name of Kingstown for a populous new settlement that was beginning to emerge on the cliffs to the east of old Dunleary village above a newly built cross-channel port. These historic events are recorded on the stone obelisk that still stands on the harbour front opposite Carlisle Pier.

COMING OF THE RAILWAY

The prestigious new harbour greatly enhanced the attraction of Kingstown as a desirable residential location. Many people who previously lived and worked in Dublin decided to follow the fashion set by the gentry in the previous century: to reside near the sea and travel to the city daily for their business. The coastal strip from Kingstown to Dublin soon began to attract a steadily increasing population and this prompted a group of Dublin bankers to propose the building of Ireland's first railway line, the Dublin & Kingstown Railway. Work began in April 1833 and, after a little over eighteen months, on 17 December 1834, a

frequent and profitable service of passenger trains was introduced on the line. The new suburban rail service was a further boost to Kingstown and the population of the town and its hinterland grew exponentially in the following decades.

Within a few years of the opening of the railway, Kingstown had grown to a sizeable centre. By 1839 shopping in its main

1834 painting of Dublin & Kingstown Railway viewed from Blackrock looking towards Williamstown and Dublin

street, George's Street, was well developed and included '9 vintners, 5 shoemakers, 10 grocers and provisioners, 3 victuallers, 5 bakers, 4 dairies, 2 carpenters, 7 drapers, 2 plumbers, 2 painters, 2 surgeons and an apothecary, together with a saddler, a stationer, a tallow chandler, a hairdresser, a cooper, a dyer, a gun maker, a bell hanger and a painter of miniatures.' By 1853, when the town had a population of about 10,500, Kingstown was the mail packet station of Dublin, to which it was linked by the new railway. George's Street, about half a mile in length, already had some seventy avenues, terraces and parades of new housing by that time.

Carlisle Pier
Kingstown
with George
IV memorial in
the 1890s

KINGSTOWN TOWNSHIP

After the opening of the railway in 1834, a number of wealthy inhabitants decided to avail of the Town Improvements Act 1828 and establish a township that year to develop and improve the area. Kingstown was the first district in County Dublin to avail of this government act, which included powers for 'the paving, watching, lighting, regulating and otherwise improving the town of Kingstown'. In 1855 the village of Glasthule was added to the township and, by an act of 1861, the management of the roads and bridges in the area were transferred from the Grand Jury to the Kingstown Town Commissioners.

The most significant architectural achievement of the Commissioners was the erection, in 1880, of the Town Hall, a Venetian-style palace with a handsome clock tower. It was designed by J L Robinson, who was also responsible for the fine granite façade of the former post office building adjoining the Town Hall, which is now integrated into the new County Hall, the administrative headquarters of Dún Laoghaire–Rathdown County Council. The commissioners took many initiatives during the nineteenth century to establish an elegant Victorian town facing the magnificent harbour. In the 1890s they acquired a disused quarry and turned it into the People's Park that contained two attractive cast-iron fountains, a handsome gate lodge and a large shelter which became the Park Tea Rooms. A variety of municipal buildings was also erected, including a fire station, a storehouse and stable for horses, a public wash-house and public baths.

In 1901, as a monument to Queen Victoria, the Kingstown Town Commissioners erected a wonderful cast-iron extravaganza in the form of a dome which they named the Victoria Fountain. It was recently refurbished and stands facing the beautiful façade of the original Dublin & Kingstown Railway terminus, which is now

Martello Tower at Seapoint, now a popular Blue Flag bathing place

occupied by Brasserie na Mara. Another notable facility provided by the commissioners in 1903 was the Pavilion, which stood in its own gardens and was very popular until it was unfortunately burned down in 1915. The Pavilion was an intricate, galleried structure with four viewing turrets and contained a number of tearooms, reading rooms and smoking rooms. It was used for concerts, dances and a variety of entertainment and its festive architecture lent a lighter note to the town's perfect Victorian image. Outside the Pavilion on Marine Road was a small building named the Cabmen's Shelter, built in 1912. It survived until recent times being finally demolished in 1997 to make way for a modern complex housing today's Pavilion Theatre.

By the second half of the nineteenth century Kingstown was firmly established in guide books as 'the largest most popular watering place in Ireland'. Contemporary photographs consistently showed Kingstown as being truly elegant and beautifully maintained, with an air of order and spaciousness surrounding the various beautiful buildings on the harbour front and in the town. The guidebooks extolled the splendour of the royal visits, the elegant yachts and the new town but omitted to mention old Dunleary or districts like Glasthule or York Road. Local historian, Peter Pearson, in his book *Between the Mountains and the Sea*, rightly draws attention to the fact that all was not perfect in Kingstown. He has recorded that in some districts there were 'dense hives of cabins' which were inhabited by the very poor and were without proper water supply or sanitation. These areas did not have the benefit of careful planning and sound building practice. In 1844 Charles Haliday, a distinguished resident and humanitarian, campaigned to rid the town of its many hovels, but it was not until the end of the nineteenth century that new terraces of artisans' dwellings were built. Haliday found more than 144 'courts' in Kingstown, which were usually narrow yards overcrowded with small, inadequate dwellings. Off George's Street Lower there were many such dwellings, with names like Duff's Court, Fagan's Court or Ball's Court. Several outbreaks of cholera occurred and disease claimed the lives of many in the area. Haliday also made the case for a proper system of sanitation but it was not until 1894 that a full network of sewers was connected to the sewerage works at the West Pier.

♦ The suburban train service inaugurated by the Dublin & Kingstown Railway in 1834 proved so popular and profitable that a proposal soon emerged to extend the railway to Dalkey. The terrain south of Kingstown, however, was hilly and any route chosen would involve steep gradients and sharp curves. Anxious not to invest in more expensive steam engines for such a line, the Company decided for its extension to Dalkey to operate train carriages without an engine under a newly invented system of motive power based on the atmospheric principle.

The system involved the carriages being connected to a metal piston that moved within a 380mm cast-iron pipe laid between the rails in which a vacuum was created. The slot through which the connecting rod between the piston and the carriages travelled was protected by a greased leather flap. To operate the train, a pumping-house near the Dalkey terminus created a vacuum in the pipe by sucking out the air and pulling the piston and attached carriages from Kingstown to Dalkey, just as a modern vacuum cleaner sucks dust from the floors of modern homes. The route was on a rising gradient to Dalkey and the return to Kingstown was by gravity. When the train was ready to return, air was released into the vacuum pipe and the train would run rapidly downhill to Kingstown, a distance of some four kilometres.

The Atmospheric Railway was opened to Dalkey on 29 March 1844 and operated very successfully during its early years. With time it was noticed that the pumping-house was having increased difficulty in sustaining an effective vacuum to draw heavy trains uphill to Dalkey. On inspection of the vacuum pipe, it was found that rats were being attracted to the leather flaps that were being smeared with lard as a preservative. Small holes were appearing where the leather had been eaten by the hungry rats. It was not long until the vacuum pipe became so perforated that the excessive air intake was destroying the vacuum and adversely affecting the atmospheric system. Despite strenuous efforts by the Dublin & Kingstown Railway to defeat them, the rats succeeded in causing such damage that the Atmospheric Railway had to close down on 12 April 1854 – just over ten years since its opening. Its fame lives on in railway lore, as the Atmospheric Railway was the first and only line in Ireland to have been forced to close because of rats. ♦

BLACKROCK TOWNSHIP

The coastal area of Blackrock, close to, but separate from, Kingstown, was on the railway line, growing rapidly and wished to emulate its larger neighbour and become a township. The area was socially mixed and included the estate of Lord Cloncurry, the indigenous fishermen of Blackrock and Williamstown and a number of shopkeepers and publicans. The inspiration for a township came from the businessmen and shopkeepers of Blackrock village and was unsuccessfully opposed by the poorer residents of Blackrock and Williamstown. The Blackrock township was established in 1860 and its area covered the village and surrounding land. The

First atmospheric train leaving Kingstown for Dalkey on 29 March 1844

valuation threshold for franchise was low at £4, a concession to the poorer elements who had objected to the formation of the township. But a substantial change came about in 1863. As a result of numerous petitions, the much more prosperous district of Monkstown became part of the township and the valuation for the franchise was raised to £8. The political consequences were that power, which had been in the hands of the liberal and largely Roman Catholic interest, transferred to a more conservative group with a much larger Protestant presence.

DALKEY TOWNSHIP

The next area in Dún Laoghaire–Rathdown to seek local government was the coastal village of Dalkey. In 1860 the *Irish Builder* characterised Dalkey as a place comparatively neglected. It was 'still a wild barren place, a field whose apparent infertility seems, with few exceptions, to deter modern innovators and speculating capitalists from investment'. Only three years later, however, at a meeting held in the Queen's Hotel, steps were taken to provide lighting in the village and by 1867 a move was made to secure a township for Dalkey. This was motivated by alleged attempts by Kingstown to take over Dalkey, notwithstanding the fact that Dalkey itself was hoping to take in the recently formed township of Killiney. The latter, however, remained independent and an act was passed in 1867 creating the Dalkey township. The act gave the Dalkey Town Commissioners powers to build a town hall and a market house, as well as powers to erect two piers at Coliemore Harbour. In the event, Goat Castle was converted into a town hall in 1868 and today houses the Dalkey Heritage Centre.

KILLINEY AND BALLYBRACK TOWNSHIP

The Killiney & Ballybrack township had only limited powers when it was established in 1866. It is surprising that Killiney ever became a township as it had no recognisable nucleus and settlement remained scattered. The prime mover was Robert Warren, a magistrate and Deputy Lieutenant for County Dublin. He became the first chairman of the board and remained in that position for almost a quarter of a century. In 1870 powers for the supply of gas and water were adopted. Before this, the water supply was very inadequate. Ballybrack, the poorer part of the township, had to rely solely on one well. Dalkey had already applied for water from the Vartry system and had it piped to the boundary of the township to facilitate its extension to Killiney at a reasonable cost. As far as gas was concerned, the needs of the Killiney Town Commissioners were modest, as they required only enough to light a few public lamps.

By establishing townships, local elites of middle-class residents were responding to immediate needs that were not being addressed by the existing weak local government structures. The fact that the Dublin townships obtained expensive local acts of parliament shows a degree of enterprising vigour and self-confidence, and a degree of support from their future ratepayers. The areas administered by the township commissioners extended inland from the coast only to the immediate hinterland of the built-up areas, as will be seen from Map 3 (p 104). But by the end of the nineteenth century, a continuous series of townships stretching from Booterstown to Ballybrack had established local government for the first time in the suburban areas of Dún Laoghaire–Rathdown. These coastal townships were amalgamated in 1930 to form the new Borough of Dún Laoghaire.

– 9 –

SMOTHERING SUBURBANISATION

The 'railway' townships of Blackrock, Kingstown, Dalkey and Killiney were truly suburban and too far removed from Dublin to be under any threat of absorption into the city's administration. Kingstown was renamed Dún Laoghaire in 1920 and when local government was reorganised by the Irish Free State in 1930, these townships were amalgamated to form the Borough of Dún Laoghaire. The relative seclusion of the borough kept population growth low and pressure for new housing developments was not as great as that exerted on the County Borough of Dublin, the area under the control of Dublin Corporation.

LANDSCAPE TRANSFORMATION

Following the Second World War, however, Dún Laoghaire Corporation came under pressure to facilitate new housing for the growing suburban population and, particularly, to improve the housing conditions of the less privileged in the borough. Many were then living in very congested housing conditions with only basic sanitation, especially in the Blackrock, Dún Laoghaire and Glasthule areas. To cater for these needs, extensive undeveloped lands were acquired by the Corporation for local authority housing in Sallynoggin and Monkstown, while private developers were encouraged to exploit wooded and more developed lands in the

Clonkeen and Cabinteely areas for private housing. With this considerable housing expansion, the population of the Borough of Dún Laoghaire began to increase significantly from 1950.

By the 1970s the Greater Dublin Area was experiencing a steady increase in population, as more and more people from the provinces were attracted by the city's employment opportunities

Blackrock's Main Street looking towards Kingstown in the 1890s

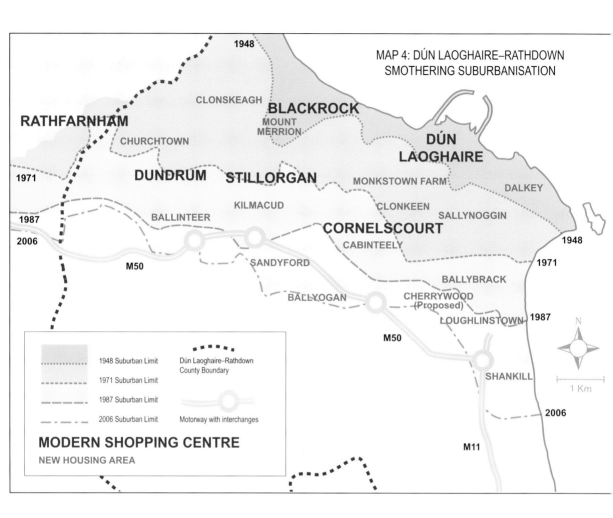

MAP 4: DÚN LAOGHAIRE–RATHDOWN
SMOTHERING SUBURBANISATION

1948

CLONSKEAGH

BLACKROCK

MOUNT MERRION

RATHFARNHAM

CHURCHTOWN

DÚN LAOGHAIRE

1971

DUNDRUM   STILLORGAN

MONKSTOWN FARM

DALKEY

1987

KILMACUD

BALLINTEER

CLONKEEN

SALLYNOGGIN

2006

CORNELSCOURT

CABINTEELY

1948

M50

SANDYFORD

1971

BALLYBRACK

BALLYOGAN

CHERRYWOOD
(Proposed)

LOUGHLINSTOWN   1987

M50

N

SHANKILL

1 Km

2006

M11

	1948 Suburban Limit		Dún Laoghaire–Rathdown County Boundary
	1971 Suburban Limit		
	1987 Suburban Limit		
	2006 Suburban Limit		Motorway with interchanges

MODERN SHOPPING CENTRE

NEW HOUSING AREA

and by standards of living higher than in rural areas. Dún Laoghaire Corporation responded to the demand for local authority housing by acquiring further undeveloped land in the southern part of its area, at Ballybrack and Shankill. Meanwhile further private housing development was encouraged by Dublin County Council in Stillorgan, Kilmacud, Churchtown and Ballinteer. By the 1980s burgeoning industrial estates were developing close to Sandyford village and these gave rise to further housing development that has today extended as far as Cherrywood. Map 4 (opposite) graphically illustrates the steady expansion of the built-up suburbs which, since 1948, have gradually obliterated many of the identifying features of the landscape in Dún Laoghaire–Rathdown.

The effects of this massive housing development over a period of some sixty years have been the virtual transformation of the landscape, the smothering of many of its features and landmarks and the concealment of most of its historic rivers and streams. As so many features of large areas of Dún Laoghaire–Rathdown were utterly changed in the recent past and have been largely forgotten, it may be useful to recall the former landscape and character of those areas developed in the past half-century.

SALLYNOGGIN / *SAIL AN CHNOCÁIN*

The first ordnance survey map of this area in 1843 shows a long row of cottages, each with its own small garden, called 'Glenagarey or Sally Noggins'. These cottages were all thatched and white-washed, and eventually were all replaced by local authority housing. One of them which became a public house known as The Thatch remained until 1972 but it was then demolished to make way for a new lounge bar. The origin of the cottages is uncertain. They were built on land belonging to the Longford and De Vesci estate in an area that was undeveloped and unfashionable. It has been suggested that the original cottages may have been built for labourers who were working on the construction of Kingstown Harbour in the nineteenth century. Further artisans' dwellings were built by Kingstown Urban District Council in 1904 and these were followed by two-storey terraced houses near the Glenageary Roundabout.

This local authority housing was the forerunner of the huge

133

public housing programme begun by Dún Laoghaire Corporation after the Second World War. This very large development in Sallynoggin, popularly known as 'the Noggin', resulted in the Rochestown Stream being placed in a culvert for its full length except for a portion within the former Dún Laoghaire Golf Club. Private housing development in the Thomastown Road area of Glenageary also caused most of the Glasthule and the Thomastown Stream to be placed underground and out of public view. The elimination of these watercourse features from the extensive area stretching from Monkstown to Killiney Hill has changed the landscape utterly.

MONKSTOWN / *BAILE NA MANACH*

Monkstown was well established as a residential area by 1843 when the first ordnance survey map of this area was published. Along Monkstown Road and the seacoast this area was, in the words of Victorian writers, 'thickly studded with handsome seats and pleasing villas'. South of the modern churches in Monkstown is the remaining gatehouse of Monkstown Castle, once the most formidable building in the area. The Rochestown Stream formerly flowed to the east of the castle and was dammed there to form what was probably a millpond to provide power for the corn mill mentioned in the 1655 *Civil Survey*. Today this stream has been totally culverted and is no longer seen by or known to the general public.

An extensive area south of Monkstown Castle, known as Monkstown Farm, was acquired by Dún Laoghaire Corporation after the Second World War for the development of public authority housing. The old farm used to be traversed by the Rochestown Stream. Another area west of the Monkstown Road, known as

134

Monkstown Valley, through which flows the Strad Brook, was developed for private housing during the 1980s. In this case the watercourse was not culverted and continues to flow as a feature through the area, although further west the same stream has been placed in a culvert between Monkstown Valley and Newtown Park.

CLONKEEN / *CLUAIN CHAOIN*

During the 1960s and 1970s extensive agricultural lands to the south-west of Monkstown and east of Foxrock Church known as Clonkeen were developed for private housing. These lands were formerly attached to the Early Christian site of Kill, which later became Dean's Grange when it belonged to the Dean of Christchurch Cathedral. That part of the lands east of Clonkeen Road is traversed by the Dean's Grange Stream, the only watercourse in Dún Laoghaire–Rathdown not originating in the Dublin Mountains. This stream rises in the vicinity of Dean's Grange Cemetery and drains the plains extending south-east from there to the sea at Killiney Bay.

In spite of all the housing development, this stream is still visible as a pleasant feature running through a linear park east of Clonkeen Road and under the Johnstown Road to the east of Cabinteely village. The Dean's Grange Stream then continues south-east through another linear park towards Kilbogget.

STILLORGAN / *STIGH LORGAN*

The busy and rather characterless Stillorgan of today has changed out of all recognition from the village that stood on the old main

The Bottle Tower in Churchtown, built as a famine relief scheme in 1741

road to Bray before the extensive redevelopment of the 1960s changed its character for ever. The old village consisted of a line of nineteenth-century cottages along the present road frontage of Stillorgan Shopping Centre car park and further small houses on one side of a steep hill that led down to the Kilmacud Stream

before its confluence with the Glaslower. There at one time stood
an old mill, below the church of St Brigid and overlooked by
the St John of God Hospital, formerly Baron Allen's Stillorgan
Castle and the site of the medieval manor. The Old Dublin Road
to Bray twisted in a detour around the church and school of St

Beranger's 1766
drawing of the
Bottle Tower,
showing a smaller
version on the left
which was built
as a dovecote

137

Brigid and continued southwards to cross the Glaslower near
Darley's Brewery, a large industrial complex whose site has been
obliterated by the N11 dual carriageway.

Today Stillorgan is noted mainly for having the first and
oldest shopping centre in Ireland, a large 24-hour leisure complex,
a multi-screen cinema and the principal grounds of Kilmacud
Crokes GAA club. To the west of Stillorgan, throughout the
areas of Kilmacud and Drumartin, extensive private housing
development took place in the 1960s and 1970s, resulting in the
Kilmacud Stream that used to run parallel to the Lower Kilmacud
Road being placed in a culvert over its full length. East of the Old
Dublin Road, local authority housing was built together with a
public library in the 1970s, while further east of the modern dual
carriageway private apartment development took place in the
1990s on lands formerly occupied by the Linden and Talbot Lodge
convalescent homes. All that remains today of the old village of
Stillorgan are the church and old school of St Brigid's Church of
Ireland parish and a small number of houses on the hill between
the traffic lights and the modern thatched public house, Stillorgan
Orchard.

CHURCHTOWN / BAILE AN TEAMPAILL

Between 1950 and 1980 the extensive area now known as
Churchtown was developed to become a densely built-up suburb of
private and local authority housing. Previously the area consisted
mainly of large dairy farms, including Landscape House owned
by the Douglas family of the well-known Dublin drapery firm
in Wexford Street, and Hazelbrook, whose dairy, owned by the
Hughes family, gave its name to the well-known ice-cream brand
of HB. Churchtown probably derived its name from the Early

Christian church of St Nahi that stood above the River Slang on the site occupied by the present church of the same name near Dundrum. Churchtown was originally reached from Dundrum by taking the small road that passes in front of St Nahi's Church of Ireland.

One of the most extraordinary structures in Dún Laoghaire–Rathdown, popularly known as the Bottle Tower, may be found in Churchtown at Whitehall, once the site of an elegant house of the same name. The tower, with a miniature companion tower, was built by Major Hall as an employment relief scheme following the Great Frost of 1740 and the forgotten famine of 1741, widely known as *Bliain an Áir* or year of the slaughter. The design of the tower was most probably inspired by barns or follies built during the 1740s at Castletown, County Kildare. The larger tower, with its external winding staircase, was probably used as a grain store, while the smaller was designed as a dovecote or pigeon house. Though sometimes called Hall's Barn, it was generally known as the Bottle Tower. Some eighteenth-century bottles were slightly cone-shaped, but the Bottle Tower closely resembles the shape of the conical towers of old glassworks, which mostly produced bottles.

RATHFARNHAM / RÁTH FEARNÁIN

Most of Rathfarnham today lies outside Dún Laoghaire–Rathdown but a small area near the village and much of its hinterland towards the Dublin Mountains belong to the county. A little to the west of the present administrative boundary stands the sixteenth-century fortified mansion of Rathfarnham Castle, which was remodelled and lavishly redecorated in the eighteenth century. The castle, built in 1585 for Archbishop Adam Loftus, Lord Chancellor of Ireland

and first Provost of Trinity College Dublin, was occupied by the Jesuit Order for almost a century when it was put up for sale in 1985. Fortunately, after considerable public pressure, the Office of Public Works agreed to purchase it, and Rathfarnham Castle is now preserved for the nation. The Castle Stream, marking the old historic boundary of Cuala and the present boundary of Dún Laoghaire–Rathdown, runs close to the grounds on its way to the Castle Golf Club, where the stream has been placed in a culvert.

The lands to the south of Rathfarnham were developed for both public and private housing during the 1970s and 1980s, effectively linking up with similar developments in Churchtown. The lands stretching west towards the Dublin Mountains contained many fine mansions built by the Dublin gentry in the eighteenth century, including Marlay House, Danesmote and Hollypark, which is now St Columba's College. These properties enjoyed fine elevated sites surrounded by trees and parklands but their lower levels were gradually developed for private housing schemes during the 1980s, changing the character of the landscape. However, a much greater landscape change has resulted from the recent construction of the M50, which has not only severed the former parklands but has facilitated a further extension of suburban housing above the line of the motorway to encroach on the Dublin Mountains.

BALLYBRACK / *AN BAILE BREAC*

The first ordnance survey map of this area in 1840 shows many new villas owned by wealthy residents on the Killiney side of the village, and cottage-style housing for the working classes on the Loughlinstown side. By the middle of the nineteenth century, Ballybrack had established itself with a growing community of

Early
suburbanisation
in the Kingstown
area viewed from
Dalkey Hill Quarries
around 1853

gardeners, carpenters and house painters who found employment with the wealthy residents of the villas and also many labourers who were employed on the Domville estate centered on Loughlinstown House. The castle, town and lands of Loughlinstown had been granted by Charles II to his attorney-general in Ireland, Sir William Domville, in the 1660s, in recognition of his services in settling all claims and disputes arising from the rebellion of 1641.

The lands of the Domville estate stretched east as far as Ballybrack and these were acquired by Dún Laoghaire Corporation in 1976 for local authority housing, industrial development and schools. The development that subsequently took place in Ballybrack has totally changed the character of the area, as the former agricultural lands have been subsumed into modern housing schemes. However, a small megalithic monument on these lands near the lower reaches of the Dean's Grange Stream has been preserved as a feature in a public housing scheme at the junction of Shanganagh Road and Killiney Hill Road, which is aptly named Cromlech Fields. Loughlinstown House, overlooking the Shanganagh River close to its confluence with the Loughlinstown River, formerly had a large enclosed garden, some woods and two small lakes. The fine building has been preserved and today houses the offices of the European Foundation.

The Ring at
Lehaunstown Point-
to-Point Races
in March 1946

Shankill / *Seanchill*

Unlike the castle of Shankill, which dates from the thirteenth century, the village is of more modern origin. A disgraceful episode in the history of the Domville estate gave rise to its existence. In the 1800s the local landlord, Sir Charles Domville, evicted his tenants when they refused to pay increased rents on winning prizes for growing the largest cabbages and finest vegetables in the area. The evicted tenants were given plots of land by a generous and charitable neighbour Mr Tilly, who owned Tillystown, which lay in a hollow behind the shops in the modern Shankill village. Cabins were set up there and in 1910 some were replaced by thirty-six granite cottages built by the local authority. A public library was added in 1912 and it served many different purposes, including that of a courthouse and temporary church.

Within the past fifty years much of the agricultural land around Shankill has succumbed to new housing developments. The area east of the Ballybrack Road and extending from the Shanganagh River along the sea cliffs to Rathsallagh was acquired for local authority housing in the 1970s and subsequently developed. A new railway station, named Shankill / *Seanchill*, was opened on the Dublin-Bray suburban line to serve this new development. Extensive lands from Corbawn Lane to the Quinn's Road area, as well as land west of the Dublin Road, were developed for private housing during the 1980s. As a consequence, Shankill is now almost totally surrounded by built-up areas and the character of the district has changed. However, the present village has improved since the former and consistently heavy road traffic was diverted from the village to the new M50 Motorway. With assistance from European Union improvement funds, the appearance of the village has been enhanced by new lighting, paving and new shops filling sites that had been derelict fifty years ago.

CABINTEELY / *CABÁN TSÍLE*

Now bypassed by the N11 dual carriageway, the village of Cabinteely was once on the main coach road from Dublin to Wicklow. Since the early nineteenth century there was a cluster of houses and cottages around the crossroads in the centre of the village, which has changed little in the past fifty years. Significant private housing development, however, has taken place on the lands surrounding Cabinteely, bringing to an end the long agricultural and sporting tradition associated with the area since the days of the medieval manor at Cornelscourt. Cabinteely village was the place where the Bray Harriers traditionally gathered for a day's hunting in the 1940s, and nearby Lehaunstown was the venue for their annual point-to-point races from 1946 to 1960. An account of Lehaunstown Races may be found in Appendix VIII.

Almost all the land east of the village has been developed for private housing. The extensive Kilbogget farm, which contained the old Killiney nursery of Watson's, was developed in the 1970s. The Dean's Grange Stream has been retained as a central feature of a linear park west of Granville Road but, after entering Kilbogget Park, it runs as a culvert as far as Wyatville Road. West of the village is Cabinteely House, where the Byrnes lived for most of the nineteenth century and until it was bought in 1933 by Joe McGrath. He was well known in connection with the bloodstock industry, Irish Hospitals' Sweepstakes and Waterford Glass and on his death in 1969, the McGrath family presented the house and part of the lands to the local authority. Thankfully, the authority preserved Cabinteely House for posterity and developed its part of the lands as a public park, with St Bride's Stream as a feature. However, the remainder of the lands was sold in 1977 for private housing development and this has resulted in further suburbs replacing former farming lands around Cabinteely.

KILMACUD / *CILL MOCHUDA*

The large houses and extensive farms that formerly comprised the hinterland west of Stillorgan village were gradually sold to developers in the 1950s and 1960s as pressure increased in the Greater Dublin area for more homes, both public and private. Former farms and estates stretching as far back as Dundrum and beyond, with the notable exception of the open farm now managed by the Airfield Trust, were transformed into new housing schemes that completely changed the landscape. The rural atmosphere that had survived into the 1950s dissolved within two decades to

Cabinteely Village in the 1940s as *Bray Harriers* gather for a day's hunting. Their Master, Michael O'Brien of Lehaunstown House, is on the white horse.

be replaced by the extensive suburbanisation of land previously reserved for agricultural use.

Many of the former villages in the area, such as Goatstown and Churchtown, were gradually absorbed and smothered by the new suburbanised development. The Kilmacud Stream, which originated in the former lakes of Lakelands, was also a casualty, as it was placed in a culvert for its total length as far as the Glaslower at Stillorgan. Its tributaries have also had to be culverted since they traversed lands later developed for the Stillorgan and Sandyford industrial estates. Indeed, this now burgeoning industrial complex has brought about a complete transformation of the landscape. From what were grazing lands in the 1950s, a modern industrial town, complete with shops, apartments and even a private hospital, has grown. This massive development has also caused the Glaslower to be placed underground from Sandyford village through the industrial estates as far as Brewery Road, causing problems which will be discussed in the next chapter.

Ballinteer /*Baile an tSaoir*

Stretching south-west from Dundrum towards Ticknock in the Dublin Mountains was one of the last undeveloped areas to have been smothered by suburbanisation. The area previously contained large houses and adjoining farmlands, such as Wyckham, Lundford Park and Gortmore. Pressure from developers enticed the owners of these estates to part with their lands from the 1970s onwards and today the area, which is now contiguous to the M50 Motorway and its link roads, is scarcely recognisable compared to the rural tranquillity that prevailed here fifty years ago.

Yet in spite of development, some redeeming features survive in the Ballinteer area. The handsome house Wyckham

146

was acquired by Simpson's Hospital in 1925 and survives today as a home for the elderly. Lundford Park was acquired by Wesley College in 1963 and is used as the headmaster's house in the fine school complex for 600 pupils that has since been built in the grounds there. A new all-Irish primary school, *Scoil Naithí*, was opened in Ballinteer in the 1970s and a new Church of St John the Evangelist was built to serve the rapidly growing population of the new housing schemes. Finally, Gortmore was acquired by the Carmelite Fathers in 1994 and its name was changed to *Gort Mhuire*; it is now a centre of spirituality. The elaborate Victorian house has been retained as a residence for the friars and the magnificent gardens with their fountains, artificial lake, bridges, boathouse, walled gardens and sham castle are still being looked after with great care.

CHERRYWOOD / *COILL NA SILÍNÍ*

Local historian Peter Pearson records that, following the demise of the church at Rathmichael in the seventeenth century, a new glebe, Cherrywood House, was selected in 1751 and was owned by the parish until 1860. This glebe probably gave its name to the most recently developed area in Dún Laoghaire–Rathdown, lying between the N11 and the M50 Motorway west of Loughlinstown. Close to the Wyatville Interchange, this major complex of offices and apartments overlooks the valley of the Shanganagh River near its confluence with the Loughlinstown River. The complex, which in turn is overlooked by the Early Christian site at Tully with its two ancient crosses, is expanding rapidly. Shortly it is to be served by an extension from Sandyford of the *Luas* Green Line from St Stephen's Green in Dublin.

The M50 Motorway, a short distance to the west of

THE LOUGHLINSTOWN CAMP 1795–98

♦ The French Revolution of 1789 had an unsettling effect on Ireland. It inspired the foundation in 1791 of the United Irishmen to pursue Wolfe Tone's inspirational claim that it would be possible to overcome the country's problems only if Catholics, Protestants and Dissenters came together and if Ireland broke the connection with England. It also gave rise to mounting unrest in the English establishment in Ireland who feared the long-held belief that 'He who is to England win, must through Ireland come in.' Indeed, it was quite conceivable that the French could invade through Ireland and that the invasion could take place along the coast near Dublin.

Loughlinstown was chosen as a strategic location from which to guard the coastal approaches. Colonel George Napier, who was put in charge of defensive operations, advised that the best place for a defence camp was the high ground of Lehaunstown and Loughlinstown overlooking Killiney Bay. A great military camp was established here in 1795 on land lying to the north of what is now the Wyatville interchange on the M50 Motorway. The camp covered an area of some 120 acres in rows of tents and wooden huts and provided for about 4000 soldiers. There were special kitchens with large stoves that could boil sixty kettles simultaneously. In 1796 the entire camp marched to Bantry Bay in the space of three days to try to prevent the French from landing there. In the event, very bad weather prevented the landing.

Various military manoeuvres were carried out to train the soldiers and every Monday a large market was held there where country people came to sell their produce. Many entertainments, balls and military reviews were held at the camp and people flocked there for such occasions. A temporary ballroom was specially erected there for dancing. At that time people tended to flock to events of public entertainment, as evidenced by the Great Pig Hunt hosted by the owner and editor of the *Dublin Evening Post,* John Magee, in 1789. That event is described in Appendix VII.

For the defence of the camp at Loughlinstown Major La Chaussée, a Frenchman in the English army, prepared a report on Killiney Bay to advise on how it should be defended. Among his many recommendations were that batteries should be constructed along the coast, that guns should be set up near the cliffs, that hedges and ditches parallel to the shore should be destroyed, and that the country houses should be fortified. Of course, no invasion of Dublin took place at that time, and after the 1798 rebellion the camp was dismantled. ♦

148

Cherrywood, has changed the landscape radically. Forming an arc around Dublin's southern suburbs as far as the M11 at Shankill, it has cut a deep scar across the top of Marlay Park demense, below Ticknock and the village of Sandyford and across the top of Leopardstown Racecourse. It traverses the site of the fifteenth-century Carrickmines Castle, a matter that caused considerable controversy until a compromise was reached to preserve a remaining ruin within a roundabout at the Carrickmines Interchange. A regrettable consequence of the extension of the M50 Motorway is that encouragement has been given to developers to continue expanding housing schemes beyond the motorway to the west, encroaching still further on the countryside in the foothills of the Dublin Mountains.

– 10 –

RIVERS AND STREAMS TODAY

In Dún Laoghaire–Rathdown there are about thirty rivers and streams between the River Dodder in the north and the River Dargle in the south. These are shown on Map 5 (p 152) and a full list is given in Appendix V. With much of the county now developed and suburbanised, many of these old watercourses are no longer visible. They have been placed underground or are out of sight or have been absorbed into the main urban drainage system. Most are now unknown or, at best, considered to be no longer relevant.

EARLY HISTORIC RELEVANCE

From earlier chapters we have seen how very relevant the rivers and streams were to the everyday lives of most people who inhabited Dún Laoghaire–Rathdown since about 3340 BC. The following is a brief recapitulation. The earliest Mesolithic people who lived on Dalkey Island used the nearest rivers along the coast to explore the interior first in search of food and later seeking temporary shelter. As shown by archaeological evidence, these first explorers of the county travelled up the Shanganagh River system from Killiney Bay and along the River Doddder from Dublin Bay to discover the Slang and Owendoher Rivers.

When the first Neolithic farmers began to open up the landscape by clearing woodlands to create fields, their first settlements were along the rivers and streams, as well as on the coastline. These early farmers built enormous stone tombs, known as megaliths, for their dead, and most are in close proximity to a river or stream. Bronze Age burial sites have been found by the Owendoher River, as well as along the Glaslower and the Dean's Grange Stream. In pre-history, rivers and streams clearly provided the first pathways for the exploration and early cultivation of the area we now know as Dún Laoghaire–Rathdown.

With the coming of Christianity and the exploitation of dairy cattle farmers lived in circular *ráth* compounds above the 200m contour, but the monastic churches were located in the valleys of the rivers and streams, probably near the important arteries of communication. Most of the Early Christian sites of major importance were located near watercourses or on the coast and they gave rise to the growth of the first small villages.

RELEVANCE TO ANGLO-NORMANS

When the Anglo-Normans invaded in the twelfth century, they superimposed the Norman manorial system of landholding on their newly conquered territory. The new lords had a preference for sites close to established Early Christian sites for their manors, from which they controlled both village and parish. Unlike the *ráthanna* of Gaelic Ireland, Norman manors were located below the 200m contour on good agricultural land. Almost all were at sites either on or close to rivers and streams. From the thirteenth century, however, the more powerful lords began to build stone castles as a better defence against the increasing frequency of raids by the dispossessed Irish. Significantly, the first stone castle in Dún Laoghaire–Rathdown was built on the *drom* above the River Slang at Dundrum. During the fourteenth century, two further

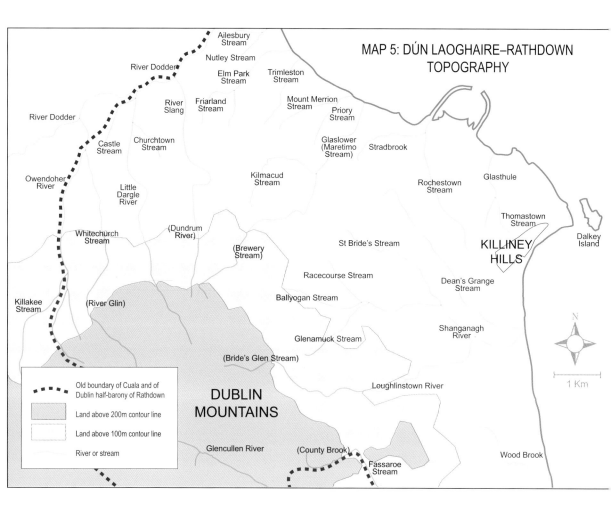

MAP 5: DÚN LAOGHAIRE–RATHDOWN TOPOGRAPHY

Old boundary of Cuala and of Dublin half-barony of Rathdown

Land above 200m contour line

Land above 100m contour line

River or stream

stone castles were built near the Ballyogan Stream at Carrickmines and on the river at Shanganagh.

MEDIEVAL RELEVANCE

Towards the end of the fifteenth century, as the area under the control of the Dublin administration was shrinking due to continual

152

attacks by the so-called 'Irish enemies', an English enclave was proclaimed to be known as The Pale. Its boundaries were defined and within the area of Dún Laoghaire–Rathdown defensive double ditches were built. In the two sections of the Pale discovered in the county strategic use in defence was made in both cases of watercourses, the Glaslower and the Ballyogan Stream.

The first map of County Dublin published by William Petty in 1685 showed additional castles built in the area of Dún Laoghaire–Rathdown. Four of these had been built along the Shanganagh River system, indicating the importance of that watercourse in defence. The relative stability of the area in the late seventeenth and early eighteenth centuries encouraged the exploitation of water power to develop proto-industries. Small mills later developed into larger mills during the eighteenth century providing much employment at Kilternan, Stillorgan, Dundrum and Rathfarnham.

WATER POWER FOR INDUSTRIES

With increasing technical knowledge during the nineteenth century, water power was harnessed for wide manufacturing and service purposes. Paper mills, cloth mills, a cotton mill and a laundry mill operated on the Owendoher River and Whitechurch Stream, while there were four mills at Rathfarnham and another four, as well as an iron works, at Dundrum on the River Slang. On the Glaslower at Stillorgan a brewery operated for over 100 years and at Kilternan on the Loughlinstown River a paper mill and a cotton mill were working in the eighteenth and nineteenth centuries. Further down the same river, at Ballycorus, water was used in a lead works by the Mining Company of Ireland.

However, following the Act of Union of 1801, circumstances

conspired to undermine these early industries and many of them were unable to withstand the competition of larger English concerns. With the development of steam and especially electricity as forms of power in the first half of the twentieth century, the use of water for industrial power declined. Rivers and streams became less critical in choosing sites for new industries and gradually the concentration of industrial activity along the watercourses of Dún Laoghaire–Rathdown diminished. The last mill at Dundrum, on the site of the medieval manor, was transformed in 1876 into the Manor Mill Laundry, which finally closed in 1943. Its site was recently absorbed into Dundrum Town Centre.

TRANSFORMATION

The concentration of large mills and industrial plants along the lower reaches of rivers and streams at Rathfarnham, Dundrum and Stillorgan over a period of time contributed to the development of nucleated settlements at these locations. By the beginning of the twentieth century each had become an established village serving mainly agricultural communities supplying produce to the growing city of Dublin. As the city expanded beyond the canals in the first half of the twentieth century to provide better housing for inner-city dwellers, pressure was exerted by property developers on owners of farms and estates in Dún Laoghaire–Rathdown to sell their lands for supplementary housing, both public and private.

By 1950 rapid changes had begun to take place throughout those areas in the vicinity of Rathfarnham, Dundrum, Stillorgan, Monkstown and Sallynoggin as former farms and estates were transformed into new housing schemes that changed the landscape utterly. The rural atmosphere that had survived until the 1950s south of the River Dodder and inland from the old built-up areas along the coast, dissolved within two decades to be replaced by extensive suburbanisation. The rivers and streams, no longer regarded as important, were absorbed into the drainage of the many uncoordinated housing schemes rapidly being completed during the second half of the twentieth century. Many of the smaller streams were put into storm water pipes connected to the nearest main drainage outflow and some of the larger rivers were placed in culverts, with little apparent thought given to exceptional flood conditions or even to the significantly reduced natural absorption qualities of the extensive concreted areas in the new housing schemes that were replacing the former fields.

DRAINAGE AND FLOODING

To this day, rivers and streams whether over or underground are still the natural rainfall runoffs in their catchment areas and have to be respected for the essential geographic function they serve. A flood-free suburban environment has not been assured in Dún Laoghaire–Rathdown since some watercourses have been placed in culverts. In many instances over the past half-century, former rivers and streams have been unduly restricted within their culverts and have been unable to carry the greatly increased water volumes arising in the aftermath of lengthy periods of sustained rainfall.

In December 1954 torrential rains caused disastrous flooding in the North Strand area of Dublin, when the River Tolka burst its banks and swept away the Dublin–Belfast mainline railway bridge. It was expected at the time that, following the culverting of many small streams in Dún Laoghaire–Rathdown, the area south of Dublin would not be similarly affected. Yet the volume of water running off the Mount Merrion housing estates was so great that the culverted Trimleston Stream was totally unable to cope. Both the old Dublin–Bray main road near St Helen's and the coastal Merrion Road at Trimleston were under feet of water, totally disrupting road communications.

Section of newly-constructed major link road washed away by the Whitechurch Stream at Taylor's Lane near Rathfarnham on 22 June 2007

HURRICANE CHARLEY 1986

In August 1986, following the twenty-four-hour downpour caused by Hurricane Charley, the flooded River Dodder was unable to cope with the huge volumes of water being disgorged by the culverts

on the lower reaches of both the Little Dargle and Slang Rivers, resulting in severe flooding in the Rathfarnham and Dundrum areas. On that occasion in 1986, the whole surface drainage system became overloaded. The River Dodder continued to rise inexorably until it left its natural channel at no less than thirteen points, beginning at Lower Dodder Road, Rathfarnham. Near Ballsbridge, twenty-five cubic metres a second were estimated to have flowed down Anglesea Road. As one cubic metre of water weighs one ton, in round figures twenty-five tons of water moved past every second!

Far from confining itself to the low-lying banks of the river, the water rampaged through gardens and houses in districts as far away as Sandymount, revealing the extent of the River Dodder's natural flood plain. In all, some 400 properties were flooded, flood being defined as an inundation of downstairs or basement floor area. Over two metres of water were recorded in some cases. In 1987 the cost of making good the damage to the river banks, the weirs and parklands alone was estimated at about €1m, while insurance claims for the property damaged totalled some €8m.

On a lesser, though no less damaging, scale the Strad Brook, Rochestown and Glasthule Streams that had been largely placed in culverts also became overloaded and erupted through manholes to flood houses and roads. Even the Glaslower, which had partially been placed in culvert at that time, overflowed its natural banks because proper provision had not been made for the drainage of water running off newly developed housing schemes in its extensive catchment area. More recently, in 1999, due to problems associated with new drainage works, serious flood damage was caused to shops and other premises in Glasthule village.

♦ Some innovative adjustments were made by Dún Laoghaire–Rathdown County Council and the former Dublin County Council and Dún Laoghaire Corporation to the overall drainage scheme during the past half century to try and cope with floodwater overflows. Artificial links have been constructed over the years between some natural watercourses to divert excessive water volumes from one catchment area to another. For example, use was made of the nineteenth-century Mill Stream south of Rathfarnham to direct water from the Owendoher River to the Whitechurch Stream. A similar man-made link was constructed early in the 1960s to connect the Nutley, Elm Park and Trimleston Streams, in order to prevent large outflows of water from the grounds of RTÉ and UCD from flooding the suburban railway line at Merrion during times of heavy rainfall.

From 1971 to 1973, a much more innovative link was built by the former Dublin County Council to connect the Glaslower and Kilmacud Streams at Stillorgan with the Dean's Grange Stream near Clonkeen. This was a unique achievement, as it was defying the geographical principles that confine rivers within their natural catchment areas and do not provide for water flowing over a natural watershed into another catchment area. The former Dublin County Council achieved their objective by constructing an overflow chamber at Stillorgan from which a pipe connects to a 1500mm wide underground culvert that travels from Upper Kilmacud along the natural contour for a distance of some 3km as far as Clonkeen. This artificial stream is unique in Dún Laoghaire–Rathdown as, contrary to natural geophysical conditions, it crosses a watershed between two natural catchment areas and is capable of redistributing flood overflows from one to the other. Excess floodwaters from the more extensive catchment areas of the Glaslower and Kilmacud Streams that flow north-east into Dublin Bay may now be sent by this unique artificial stream over the natural watershed into the less extensive catchment area of the Dean's Grange Stream to flow south-east instead into Killiney Bay. The advantages of its use, however, are limited because of separate instances of flooding occurring in the Dean's Grange Stream catchment area. ♦

Rathfarnham Flooding 2007

Serious flooding problems persist to our own day. A hidden stream wreaked havoc as recently as 22 June 2007, when a cloudburst following a thunderstorm caused severe flooding in the Rathfarnham area and washed away part of a new main link road at Taylor's Lane. The Whitechurch Stream, known locally as the River Glin, rose over two metres in its narrow channel, overflowed on to the Whitechurch Road, and rushed down into low-lying houses in Grange Park. Flood waters flowed through the front gardens, ground floors and back gardens of many houses, destroying everything in their path. Near the entrance to the Grange Golf Club at Taylor's Lane, the torrent destroyed a road bridge over the Whitechurch Stream and washed away a section of a newly-constructed major link road. Residents and onlookers were caught unawares by the suddenness of the rise in the water level of the hidden Whitechurch Stream and were horrified by the frightening speed and power of the flood waters. Cars parked at the entrance to the golf club were under three metres of water at the height of the flooding. This latest occurrence made quite clear that inadequate provision had been made for exceptional flood water levels in the recently-built culvert under the new road.

Stillorgan Flooding 2007

Less than a month later, on 17 July 2007, another cloudburst following a thunderstorm caused the Glaslower to burst its banks at a number of locations near Stillorgan. Houses and commercial premises in the Stillorgan, Sandyford, Leopardstown and Blackrock areas were damaged in flash flooding following a torrential downpour. The housing areas most affected included

159

Orpen Dale and Orpen Green in Stillorgan and Avoca Park and Avondale in Blackrock. Flood waters up to half a metre deep flowed through a number of houses and the intensity of the floods caused several manholes to burst open and turn into fountains. The speed with which the flash floods erupted from a nearby hidden stream was very frightening, especially for new residents in the area who were quite unaware of the potential danger of the Glaslower, which drains an extensive area of the foothills of the Dublin Mountains.

It is interesting that since 2003 Dún Laoghaire–Rathdown County Council have been receiving consulting engineers' advice on what it describes as the Maretimo Stream in order to eliminate or substantially reduce 'the unacceptable frequency of flooding in the Carysfort area of Blackrock'. However, it was only after this most recent serious flooding that it was stated that plans were to be brought forward to the council in September 2007 aimed at improving drainage in the Glaslower catchment area.

Future Drainage Policy

Since the turn of the century, Dún Laoghaire–Rathdown County Council has been studying ways of reducing the risks of frequent flooding in all areas of the county. The water services department participated in the Greater Dublin Strategic Drainage Study, which produced recommendations for various elements of both foul and surface water drainage across the region. The department is now implementing new policies that integrate and fully comply with EU directives in relation to water, including the Water Framework directive of 2000.

One of these new policies is to avoid placing small rivers and streams in culverts wherever possible. In some cases the department may insist that culverts be removed to return the stream to its natural state. Screens at the mouths of existing culverts have been reconstructed to improve debris removal and to reduce the potential of blockages. Sustainable urban drainage systems (SUDS) are now incorporated into all new planning proposals. These systems enable the rainfall run-off in new impermeable areas to reciprocate that of an existing greenfield site. This would be approximately equivalent to two litres per second per hectare.

Developers must now incorporate SUDS proposals in their planning applications. Larger sites would include the creation of supplementary 'off-line' ponds or wetlands to retain, restrict

The Glaslower in flood at Carysfort Park near Blackrock on 17 July 2007

and treat the impermeable run-offs from the site. Other methods may include the provision of swales, ditches and filter drains to achieve the same objectives, while smaller developments may use porous paving and soakaways. Treatment of rainfall run-off from developed areas is highly important to achieve the necessary water quality for the receiving rivers and for bathing areas along the coast.

Dún Laoghaire–Rathdown County Council is making progressive changes in its drainage policy to manage the existing problems and future climate change. The council is now intent on avoiding future repetition of frequent incidents of flooding in the areas within its jurisdiction.

INFLUENCE ON SETTLEMENT PATTERN

Apart from their important drainage functions, the rivers and streams have also had a significant influence on the modern shaping of Dún Laoghaire–Rathdown. We have seen how important the various rivers and streams were from the earliest times for the exploration and later settlement of people, and how many of the major Early Christian monastic sites and the Anglo-Norman manors were established near running water.

Over time, four main groups of rivers and streams in the county attracted continuity of settlement:

1. The Owendoher and Whitechurch fast-flowing watercourses above Rathfarnham
2. The River Slang, especially near its bend in a valley below a ridge at Dundrum
3. The Glaslower and Kilmacud Streams around their confluence at Stillorgan

162

4.   The Shanganagh and Loughlinstown Rivers, at their
        Cherrywood confluence

The sea coast also attracted continuity of settlement, especially near the mouths of the Glaslower and Rochestown Streams, as well as on the promontory where the modern town of Dalkey is located.

     All four groups attracted some prehistoric settlement. Three of them attracted major Early Christian settlements at Cruagh on the Owendoher River, at Balally near the River Slang, and at Tully near the Shanganagh River. Significantly, the same three rivers, together with the Glaslower, were locations chosen by the Anglo-Normans to set up their medieval manors:

1.   At Rathfarnham near the confluence of the Owendoher
        and Dodder Rivers
2.   At Dundrum on a ridge above the bend in the River
        Slang
3.   At Stillorgan above the confluence of the Glaslower and
        Kilmacud Streams
4.   At Cornelscourt, Kilgobbin and Kilternan on tributaries
        of the Shanganagh River

Another manor was established at Dalkey, a major Early Christian site close to Dalkey Island, where evidence was found of the earliest mesolithic human settlement in Dún Laoghaire–Rathdown.

     From the earliest maps in the seventeenth century it is clear that castles, houses, watermills and settlements were largely concentrated in the catchment areas of the four main groups of watercourses. By the late eighteenth and early nineteenth centuries many early industries developed along the four watercourse groups, especially the Owendoher River and the Whitechurch Stream.

These gave rise to the growth of small concentrated population settlements but, as the fortunes of small Irish industries began to decline in the face of competition from larger English industries in the nineteenth century, these settlements were gradually abandoned.

The opposite happened along the coast from Dublin as far as Dalkey, following the building of an 'asylum harbour' at Kingstown and a railway linking that town with Dublin. In the mid-nineteenth century new administrative townships were established from Blackrock to Killiney to cater for the needs of the growing population. It was significant that the cores of these townships were at Blackrock, the site of an old fishing village at

New suburban
housing
encroaches on
the twelfth-century
Kilgobbin Cross

the mouth of the Glaslower; at Kingstown, beside the old fishing village of Dunleary in a creek below the medieval Monkstown Castle on the Rochestown Stream; and at Dalkey, the site of a medieval manor.

EMERGENCE OF MODERN CENTRES

With the continuity of settlement in the main river groups and the growth of strong new coastal communities in the nineteenth century, it was not surprising that commercial, religious and social activities tended to concentrate on the historic centres of these settlements in the twentieth century. As the Dublin suburbs began to expand rapidly south of the River Dodder from 1950 onwards, new commercial centres to service the growing population were built almost without exception at the older historic centres that had already been established over many centuries. In fact, the largest modern shopping centres built in Dún Laoghaire–Rathdown over the past fifty years were located at Rathfarnham, Dundrum, Stillorgan, Cornelscourt, Blackrock and Dún Laoghaire. The first four were the locations of medieval manors near rivers and streams, while the last two were near the old fishing villages at the mouths of watercourses.

It is not being asserted that rivers and streams consciously determined the locations of the six largest modern commercial centres in Dún Laoghaire–Rathdown, but that over time they did have a significant influence on the concentration of population settling in these locations. Despite the fact that many rivers and streams had been smothered by suburbanisation in the second half of the twentieth century, people historically had become accustomed to gravitate towards particular centres for their regular needs and unwittingly had accepted the accumulated wisdom

BOOTERSTOWN MARSH

♦ A fortunate consequence of the construction of the Dublin & Kingstown Railway across part of Merrion Strand was the creation of a wild bird sanctuary now known as Booterstown Marsh. It is the only remaining salt marsh lagoon in Dún Laoghaire–Rathdown and provides a unique and accessible natural habitat within an urban setting.

The building of the railway in 1834 on a raised stone-faced embankment that cut across Dublin Bay between Merrion and Blackrock separated the tidal lagoons from the sea. The original lagoons along this coastline were eventually filled in, with the exception of the small lake in Blackrock Park. From the middle of the nineteenth century, the marsh area was grazed or cultivated and some cultivated ridges can still be seen at the eastern end when water levels recede in summertime. Much of the lagoon was drained for growing crops during the First World War and, at the western end of the marsh, allotments for vegetable growing were organised in the 1940s by the Mount Street Club.

After the Second World War the land fell into disuse. Marsh vegetation gradually reclaimed the arable land and the lagoon reformed itself, returning much of the salt marsh to its original state. When the new RTÉ centre and the UCD campus were built in the 1960s, the Nutley, Elm Park and Trimleston Streams were placed in culvert and linked together by an artificial channel on the inland side of the railway line, so that much of the water from these streams was discharged into the Booterstown Marsh. This has resulted in a large volume of fresh water entering the salt marsh, creating a brackish lagoon fed with both fresh and salt water.

In 1971 An Taisce acquired Booterstown Marsh from the Pembroke estate and now manages the property as a protected environment with heritage significance. As a bird sanctuary it serves as a resting stop for migrating waterfowl and is internationally important as a feeding and roosting area in winter for ducks, geese and waders. Being the last fresh and salt-water natural habitat in Dún Laoghaire–Rathdown, the marsh deserves preservation not only for community enlightenment but also for the benefit of species such as moorhens, reed buntings, sedge warblers, teal, snipe, lapwings, as well as various waders and seabirds. ♦

of the past by continuing to frequent centres located on the old watercourses.

It could well be argued, of course, that one of the four main groups of watercourses, the Shanganagh and Loughlinstown Rivers, did not succeed like the others in attracting growing population settlements and that the significant promise of these rivers has not so far been realised. That is true, probably because of the failure in the nineteenth century of the paper and cloth mills at Kilternan and the decline in demand for lead from Ballycorus after the First World War. Similarly, the settlements in the valleys of the Owendoher River and Whitechurch Stream around Rockbrook were not sustained due to the nineteenth-century decline of Irish industries, as well as the emergence of steam and electricity as alternative power sources to water in the twentieth century.

CONTINUING INFLUENCE

Powerful influence is, however, still being exerted by the rivers and streams on the future development and shape of Dún Laoghaire–Rathdown. It is not without significance that one of the first acts of the newly created county council in 1991 was to choose Dundrum as its 'second county town'. This was the site of the ancient Neolithic settlement in the River Slang valley, beside the major Early Christian site at Balally and the later medieval manor. It was also the location of the first Anglo-Norman stone castle at Dundrum and of numerous water-powered industries and their supporting settlements in the eighteenth and nineteenth centuries. A further significant development is that the county council is planning to locate a 'third county town' near Cherrywood, not far from the megalithic monuments of pre-history, close to the major Early Christian site at Tully and within sight of the ruins of the Anglo-

167

Norman castle in the Shanganagh River valley. When this third town has been established, we will truly be able to assert that all the major rivers and streams have had a profound influence on the history and shaping of the modern Dún Laoghaire–Rathdown.

MEGALITHIC TOMBS
IN DÚN LAOGHAIRE–RATHDOWN

	TOWNLAND	TOMB TYPE	ADJACENT RIVER OR STREAM
1	Kilmashoge	Portal (collapsed)	Whitechurch Stream
2	Kilmashoge	Wedge	Kilmashoge Mountain at 229m
3	Taylor's Grange	Portal (part of)	Little Dargle River
4	Ballyedmonduff	Passage	Two Rock Mountain top (536m)
5	Ballyedmonduff	Wedge	Two Rock Mountain at 335m
6	Kilternan	Portal	Loughlinstown River
7	Brennanstown	Portal	Ballyogan Stream
8	Lehaunstown	Wedge	Loughlinstown River
9	Ballybrack	Portal	Shanganagh River
10	Shankill	Wedge	On Carrickgollogan Hill

APPENDIX II A

EARLY CHRISTIAN CHURCHES
IN DÚN LAOGHAIRE–RATHDOWN

	TOWNLAND	SITE	ADJACENT RIVER OR STREAM
1	Rathfarnham	Church and graveslabs	River Dodder
2	Churchtown	Church	River Slang
3	Whitechurch	Church and graveslabs	Whitechurch Stream
4	Kilmashoge	Church and graveslab	Whitechurch Stream
5	Balally	Major Church and enclosure	River Slang
6	Stillorgan	Church	Glaslower
7	Newtown	Church	Glaslower
8	Carrickbrennan	Church	Rochestown Stream
9	Kill-of-the-Grange	Major Church and graveslab	Dean's Grange Stream
10	Dalkey	Church and graveslab	Near coast
11	Dalkey Island	Major Church and graveslabs	Island site
12	Cruagh	Major Church and round tower	Owendoher River
13	Kilgobbin	Church, graveslabs and bullaun	Ballyogan Stream
14	Killiney	Major Church and graveslab	Near coast
15	Kilternan	Major Church and bullaun	Loughlinstown River
16	Lehaunstown	Major Church and graveslabs	Shanganagh River
17	Rathmichael	Major Church, enclosure, round tower and graveslabs	Loughlinstown River
18	Shankill	Church	Near coast
19	Shanganagh	Church	Wood Brook
20	Ballyman	Church and graveslabs	Fassaroe Stream

APPENDIX II B

EARLY CHRISTIAN CROSSES
IN DÚN LAOGHAIRE–RATHDOWN

	SITE	CROSS TYPE	LOCATION
1	Blackrock	Small on plinth	Top of Main Street
2	Jamestown	Standing (1.2m)	Stepaside Golf Course
3	Kilgobbin	High (2.4m)	On road below old church
4	Kiltuc	Small	Shankill Church grounds
5	Rathmichael	Small	In lane to old graveyard
6	Tully (West Cross)	High (2.2m)	In field opposite old church
7	Tully (East Cross)	High (2.3m)	On high plinth in roadway

APPENDIX III

CASTLES AND TOWER HOUSES
IN DÚN LAOGHAIRE–RATHDOWN

	SITE	TYPE	LOCATION
1	Bullock	Fifteenth-century replacing previous thirteenth-century	Overlooking and protecting fishing rights and harbour
2	Dalkey	Two fortified storehouses probably sixteenth century	On opposite sides of Castle Street: Goat and Archibold's Castles
3	Dundrum	Fifteenth-century replacing first thirteenth-century Anglo-Norman stone castle	On height overlooking River Slang and Dundrum Town Centre
4	Kilgobbin	Fifteenth-century tower house	Stepaside on Sandyford Road
5	Monkstown	Gate-tower and shell of thirteenth–fifteenth-century large castle	Opposite roundabout at top of Carrickbrennan Road
6	Puck's Castle	Fifteenth-century square ruin of tower house	On hillside near Rathmichael
7	Rathfarnham	Sixteenth-century fortified mansion	South of Main Street
8	Shanganagh	Fifteenth-century ruin	Off Ballybrack-Shankill Road
9	Shankill	Only 10m tower remains of thirteenth-century Anglo-Norman	Off Ferndale Road Shankill, at foot of Carrickgollogan Hill

Appendix IV

Martello Towers
from Bray to Sandymount

	Tower	Location	Present Status
1	Bray	seafront	Demolished, probably in 1880s
2	Bray	Seapoint Road	Still standing as private house
3	Bray	Ravenswell	Demolished as unsafe in 1860s
4	Shankill	Quinn's Road	Demolished as unsafe in 1906–7
5	Shanganagh	Cliffs	Never a tower, battery gone in 1815
6	Killiney	Strand Road	Now an inhabited luxury dwelling
7	Killiney	Hill Road	Still standing in private ownership
8	Killiney	South end of Vico Road	Never a tower, battery gone in nineteenth century
9	Dalkey	Island	Still standing, with battery
10	Dalkey	South of Bullock Harbour	Still standing in private grounds
11	Sandycove	on point	Now housing the Joyce Museum
12	Glasthule	Martello Avenue	Demolished in mid-nineteenth century
13	Dún Laoghaire	Crofton Road	Demolished when building railway in 1834
14	Blackrock	Seapoint	Now housing Genealogical Society of Ireland
15	Blackrock	Williamstown	Owned by Dún Laoghaire–Rathdown County Council
16	Sandymount	seafront	Still standing – was used as shop / restaurant

APPENDIX V

RIVERS AND STREAMS
IN DÚN LAOGHAIRE–RATHDOWN

	CATCHMENT AREA	RIVER (OR STREAM)	TRIBUTARIES
1	Owendoher	Owendoher River *Abhainn Dothair*	Kilakee Stream
2	Whitechurch	Whitechurch Stream (River Glin) *Glas Chill Mochióg'*	—
3	Little Dargle	Little Dargle River* *An Deargail Bheag'*	Churchtown Stream
		Castle Stream* *Glas Chaisil*	Abbey Stream
4	Slang	River Slang* (Dundrum River) *Abhainn Dhún Droma*	—
5	Elm Park	Elm Park Stream* *Glas Mhuirfin*	Friarland Stream*
		Nutley Stream* *Glas Nothaile*	Ailesbury Stream*
6	Trimleston	Trimleston Stream* *Glas Ghleann na Míne*	—
7	Priory	Priory Stream *Glas na Mainistreach*	Mount Merrion Stream
8	Brewery	Glaslower* (Maretimo Stream) *Glas Lobhar*	Kilmacud Stream*
9	Monkstown	Rochestown Stream* *Glas na Manach*	Strad Brook*
10	Glenageary	Glasthule* *Glas Tuathail*	Thomastown Stream*

	Catchment Area	River (or Stream)	Tributaries
11	Deansgrange	Dean's Grange Stream* (Monastery Stream) *Glas na Cille*	—
12	Shanganagh	Shanganagh River (Bride's Glen Stream) *Abhainn Shean Chonach*	Loughlinstown River
			St Bride's Stream
			Racecourse Stream
			Ballyogan Stream
			Glenamuck Stream
13	Crinken	Wood Brook *Glas na Coille*	—
14	County Brook	Fassaroe Stream (County Brook) *Glas an Fhásaigh Rua*	—
15	Glencullen	Glencullen River *Abhainn Ghleann Cuilinn*	—

* Wholly or partly underground in culvert

APPENDIX VI

HOLY WELLS

At the beginning of the twentieth century, County Dublin was reputed to have over a hundred holy wells at which people privately venerated a saint, or participated in a popular religious and secular assembly on a *pattern* day designated for commemorating the patron saint of the area. As Dublin inexorably extended its suburban sprawl and filled up the former countryside with urban newcomers unaware of local history or traditions, most of these former places of local veneration fell into disuse and were soon forgotten. However, some such holy wells are still remembered in Dún Laoghaire–Rathdown.

The first, where the author personally participated in a prayer ceremony early in the 1940s, was situated low down at the bottom of a steeply sloping field near the ruins of the twelfth-century church of Ballyman by the Fassaroe Stream which forms the southern border of Dún Laoghaire–Rathdown. The well was dedicated to St Kevin of Glendalough and its waters were reputed to cure abnormalities or infections in the eyes. By the 1940s public pilgrimages to this well at Ballyman had ceased but the custom of private prayer was still being practised. According to John Dalton's *History of County Dublin*, in 1838 there was an ash tree near this well 'festooned with scraps of cloth', a custom found in many countries, even in the Far East, where people believe that scraps of material can acquire virtues against sickness by proximity to a saint. Today, St Kevin's Well at Ballyman is difficult to locate as it seems to have been buried in soil.

A second holy well in Dún Laoghaire–Rathdown was close to the author's home in Seapoint, south of Blackrock. On the way

down Seapoint Avenue from Blackrock, the first turn left after the
Midway shop is named Tobernea Terrace and it leads to this holy
well. A gate on the left at the end of this roadway leads to steps
down to the foot of the sea cliffs that existed here before the Dublin
& Kingstown Railway was built in 1834. At the bottom of the
steps, one should turn left to an overgrown path leading away up
the slope towards the old well – now only a blocked arched hole
in the side of the cliff that led to the short tunnel into the well.

Liam Mac Cóil in *The Book of Blackrock* describes how
his grandmother, when very small, had visited the holy well of
Tobernea:

> My poor father used to bring us down. He hadn't what you'd
> call very strong eyes. And he'd bring a clean cloth and he'd
> bathe his eyes in the well; and bring a bit of rag, whatever
> meaning was in the rag I don't know, but the tree was full of
> rags, red rags and all classes and colours.

It would appear that Tobernea was frequented by the people of
Blackrock at least to the beginning of the twentieth century. People
from Dublin were also known to have come out to the well and
taken away with them bottles of its water. The saint to which
Tobernea was dedicated is not known but people living in the
immediate area, where the name is pronounced 'Tubber-nay',
believed it was a corruption of *Tobar Naithí* or St Nahi's Well and
was linked to *Teach Naithí* or Taney near Dundrum.

A third holy well in Dún Laoghaire–Rathdown was Lady's
Well on the seashore near Dalkey. To reach this well, it was
necessary to scramble along the rocky shore in front of a house
named *Carraig na Gréine*, latterly occupied by the Loreto Sisters,
to reach a passage leading some distance underground to the well.
Charles Leslie, a wealthy wholesale chemist who built this striking

stone-cut house around 1830, had first tried to cut off public access to the holy well but later agreed to construct a tunnel near the shore at the bottom of his grounds to preserve a right-of-way to it. Ostensibly, Charles Leslie built it so that the public could still visit the well without having to cross his land, but of course the tunnel also ensured that the hundreds of ordinary people regularly visiting Lady's Well in the ninetenth century would not be seen from the fine windows of his magnificent home. Unhappily, since the Loreto Sisters left *Carraig na Gréine*, the tunnel has been blocked up and access is no longer possible to this once popular holy well.

APPENDIX VII

THE GREAT PIG HUNT

If one takes a sharp left turn at the top of Temple Hill coming from Blackrock, one reaches Temple Crescent where on the right-hand side stands the magnificent mansion of Neptune. Here one of the most bizarre events of eighteenth-century Blackrock took place on Old Lammas Day, 12 August 1789. James Scott, first Earl of Clonmel and Chief Justice of the King's Bench lived in this fine house, one of the most impressive residences in Blackrock, which was described in *Lewis' Guide* of that time as 'remarkably elegant'.

John Magee, owner and editor of the *Dublin Evening Post*, became involved in a libel action with the 'Sham Squire', Francis Higgins, later to feature tangentially in the history of Blackrock as the betrayer of Lord Edward Fitzgerald. During the trial, James Scott, the Chief Justice, adopted a very partisan attitude and did all he could to have John Magee convicted, including harassing him with fiats, an arbitrary method of bringing people to justice at that time. Heavy legal costs were awarded against Magee and this eventually led to his imprisonment. On his release from prison, he decided to exact revenge on the Chief Justice. He set about it with a sense of humour and imagination in a way that would cause the greatest harm to Scott but the least to himself.

James Scott had expended a great deal of care and attention on Neptune. He had magnificently planted and laid out a costly pleasure garden, of which he was immensely proud. Magee knew this only too well. In some way, he managed to rent some land that had previously been used for horse-racing adjacent to Neptune, which he called Fiat Hill. He then proceeded to organise what he proclaimed in the *Dublin Evening Post* as an 'Irish Festivity or a *Lau Braugh Pleasura*' (in modern Irish this would read *Lá Breá Pléisiúrtha*). To this great event he invited the citizens of Dublin, announcing:

> The Irish Festivity or *Lau Braugh Pleasura* will commence with a Boat Race – the boats all ranged and to start from the Pier of Dunleary to a minute at 11 o'clock. At one o' clock the Ball will be kicked on Fiat Hill, the grounds adjoining James Scott, Baron Earlsfort, Premier of the Court of King's Bench, his magnificent seat at Marino, late Lord Tracton's. Dinner on the tented field at three o'clock. The Table D'Hote for ladies and gentlemen. Cudgel playing at five on a proper stage, with cool umpires to prevent ill temper and preserve good humour. At seven o'clock his worship, the Sham, will be coursed over the grounds. To close with harpers and pipers for the boys and girls.
>
> Fiat Hill will be open to every publican who engages to the steward to bring on the tented field wines good in their kind – native punch – nectar-ambrosial – nectar and provision – the best of Dublin Markets' supply.
>
> Fiat Hill is the ground lately held by Lady Osbourne and stretches from Lord Earlsfort's demesne wall along the Blackrock Road leading to Dunleary. Lady Osbourne has leased the lands in perpetuity to Magee of the Arms of Ireland, late Fiat Dungeon Cell No 4 in the New Bastille opposite the Courts of Irish Justice, Steward of the Irish Festival or *Lau Braugh Pleasura* at Dunleary, in honour of George Prince of Wales on Lammas Day.

According to an account given by Thomas O'Flanagan, a former member of the United Irishmen who was present that day and who

180

was a nonagenarian when interviewed, the whole purpose of this extravagant event was to enable Magee to be avenged on the Chief Justice, who was living at Temple Hill in magnificently planted and laid out pleasure grounds. In the fields adjoining, Magee advertised foot races, ball-kicking, running in sacks and pursuing pigs with soaped tails, which were to become the property of the winner. Thomas O'Flanagan continued:

> A fine fat boar was christened Shamado and other pigs, wearing wigs of different forms and hue, were known to personate Lord Clonmel, Daly and others of that clique. 8,000 people assembled, the great bulk of whom were supplied with porter by Magee. The pigs having been let loose burst through the fences into Lord Clonmel's pleasure grounds, followed by the mob who utterly destroyed its beauty, on which the chief justice expended several thousand pounds and many an hour of his precious time in superintending.

Magee's plan succeeded completely. Every man did justice to his entertainer's hospitality. Lord Clonmel's magnificent demesne was uprooted and left desolate the next day, exhibiting nothing but the ruins of the Great Pig Hunt.

APPENDIX VIII

LEHAUNSTOWN RACES

From 1946 to 1960 Bray Harrriers' annual point-to-point races were held at Lehaunstown in the fields surrounding the ruined site of the Early Christian church of *Tulach na nEaspag*, or Tully, near Cabinteely. Point-to-point races evolved from racing across country and have been associated traditionally with hunts and hunting. According to local historian Liam Clare, who attended Lehaunstown Races in his youth, this annual event was usually held on a Wednesday in March. It generated enormous popular interest, excitement and enthusiasm 'not just for regular racegoers, not just the hunting set, but for people from all walks of life, young and old, who walked, cycled, bussed, drove or came by train to participate in a great occasion'.

The late Michael O'Brien of Lehaunstown House, the man behind the event, became Master of the Hunt of Bray Harriers in 1943 and proposed a course for point-to-point races on his own farm. The lower grassy slopes of the furze-covered hilltop of Lehaunstown formed the 'grandstand' from which the whole course could be seen. According to Liam Clare:

> Standing on the 'grandstand', looking eastwards towards
> Killiney, you would see the horses lined up on your left
> before they thundered off to the right across Heronford Lane.
> They headed down towards Loughlinstown, turning left
> before recrossing the roadway beside Tully Church. They
> then sped northwards right to left along the ridge of Tully to
> Carrickmines, turned back along the side of the golf course

and raced past the crowd for a second time before reaching the
winning post.

The course was three and a half miles long of firm upland, stubble, grassland and ploughed fields. There were 'drop ditches' where the horses jumped onto a bank and down into a field at lower level. There were 'double banks' which meant two parallel banks had to be jumped, causing the horse to break step before jumping onto the second bank. There were 'up banks' with a high jump up but a smaller jump off. There were walls to jump and there was a stream across the course. Most of these were existing obstructions, but two 'double banks' were specially built, which involved the replacing for safety reasons of large boulders by smaller stones.

At Lehaunstown there were generally six races on the programme – a Members' Race, a Farmers' Race, an Open Maiden Race, an Open Heavyweight Race, an Open Lightweight Race and a Nomination Race to which members could nominate an entry. Owners tended to be farmers who were also hunt members. After five or six appearances at hunts, a horse got a Hunt Cert and could be entered in the point-to-point. Such an apprenticeship was necessary because of the extra fitness needed for the extended gallop. The more successful entries in the point-to-point went on to Fairyhouse Races on Easter Monday and to Punchestown Races two weeks later. Jockeys often started their careers at point-to-points and then went on to national hunt racing. Horses which won a few point-to-point races increased considerably in value. A press report of the first meeting at Lehaunstown in 1946 stated that three jockeys had participated in their first race there – Jack Doran, Tony Power, and fifteen-year-old 'Paddy' Taaffe, who later achieved great fame as Pat Taaffe.

Liam as a youngster was more interested in the sideshows than in the horse racing itself. He recalls that in 1946 there were eighty-four bookies present, with tick-tack men relaying the odds and laying off bets. 'Here's Joe, The-Man-with-the-Monkey' attracted a lot of attention, as did the Trick-of-the-Loop and the Three-Card-Trick men. Liam Clare has vivid memories of Michael O'Brien, Master of the Hunt, in green riding-gear racing past and shouting at the juveniles to keep behind the rope, before the horses would thunder past.

Lehaunstown was not just a test of horses but a major social event. Local businesses, even the pubs, in Bray closed for the afternoon, while the schools let their pupils out early or else closed down for the day. On at least one occasion, in 1947, Shankill Court was not held on the usual Wednesday as it happened to fall on the day of Lehaunstown Races. There was less general interest in these races among the residents in the Foxrock area. The local school closed for the day but in the shops, such as Findlater's or Lawlor's the chemists, it was business as usual.

The crowds travelled to Lehaunstown by train from Bray or from Harcourt Street, alighting at Carrickmines and walking from there across the fields to the course. Liam Clare remembers that, like other youngsters, he cycled from Bray to Loughlinstown and up Bride's Glen. Other racegoers came by bus to Loughlinstown and tramped from there across country to the course. Some came by car, though the parking fee was ten shillings, a huge sum in those days. Despite this cost and the fact that cars were only gradually returning to the roads after the Second World War, nearly 1,000 cars were reported as being present at the first Lehaunstown Race Meeting in 1946. The congestion that this number created after the event must have been severe, considering the narrowness of the solitary car exit by the cul-de-sac lane down from Tully Church to the Brennanstown Road at Cabinteely.

Hundreds of pedestrians and cyclists always added to the confusion after the races. Not all racegoers were from Bray or even the surrounding areas. Many people came from Dublin and its southern suburbs because of the convenient location, the interesting course and the fact that Lehaunstown Races were free of charge for everyone.

BIBLIOGRAPHY

Clare, Liam (1995): *Memories of Lehaunstown Races* (Foxrock Local History Club)

Corlett, Christiaan (1999): *Antiquities of Old Rathdown* (Wordwell, Bray)

Dickson, David (1997): *Arctic Ireland: The Great Frost of 1740-41* (White Row Press, Belfast)

Gantz, Jeffrey (transl.) (1981): *Early Irish Myths and Sagas* (Penguin Classics, London)

Givens, John (2006): *A Guide to Dublin Bay: Mirror to the City* (Liffey Press, Dublin)

Goodbody, Rob (1993): *On the Borders of the Pale* (Pale Publishing, Dublin)

Healy, Elizabeth and others (1988): *The Book of the Liffey* (Wolfhound Press, Dublin)

Holm, Poul (1986): 'The Slave Trade of Dublin, Ninth to Twelfth Centuries' in *Peritia 5*

Joyce, Weston St John (1921): *The Neighbourhood of Dublin* (2nd ed., Gill & Macmillan, Dublin)

Kennedy, Dermot (1989): *The Siege at Carrickmines Castle 1642* (Foxrock Local History Club)

Kissane, Noel (1988): *Historic Dublin Maps* (National Library of Ireland)

Mac Cóil, Liam (1981): *The Book of Blackrock* (Carraig Books, Blackrock, Co Dublin)

MacNeill, Charles (ed.) (1950): *Calendar of Archbishop Alen's Register* (RSAI, Dublin)

Moriarty, Christopher (1991): *Down the Dodder* (Wolfhound Press, Dublin)

Ó Corráin, Donnchadh (1997): 'Ireland, Wales, Man, and the Hebrides' in *The Oxford Illustrated History of the Vikings* (Oxford University Press, Oxford)

Ó Cróinín, Dáibhí (1992): 'Medieval Frontiers and Fortifications: the Pale and its Evolution' in *Dublin City & County: From Prehistory to Present* (Geography Publications, Dublin)

Ó Maitiú, Séamas (2003): *Dublin Suburban Towns 1834-1930* (Four Courts Press, Dublin)

Ó Rónáin, Maolmhuire (1936): *Dún Laoghaire agus na Ceantair Mágcuaird* (Foilseacháin Rialtais., BÁC)

Ormond, Richard (1977): *Royal Faces: 900 Years of British Monarchy* (HMSO, London)

186

Pearson, Peter (1998): *Between the Mountains and the Sea* (O'Brien Press, Dublin)

Quinn, D B (1987): '*Irish* Ireland and *English* Ireland' in *A New History of Ireland II* (Oxford)

Ryan, Christopher (2002): *Dundrum, Stillorgan and Rathfarnham* (Cottage Publications, Donaghadee)

Simmington, Robert (1945): *The Civil Survey* AD *1654-56, Vol 7: County of Dublin* (Irish Manuscripts Commission)

Simms, Anngret and Fagan, Patricia (1992): 'Villages in County Dublin: Their Origins and Inheritance' in *Dublin City & County: From Prehistory to Present* (Geography Publications, Dublin)

Simpson, Linzi (1994) 'Anglo-Norman Settlement in Uí Briúin Cualann, 1169-1350' in *Wicklow History & Society* (Geography Publications, Dublin)

Stout, Geraldine & Matthew (1992): 'Patterns in the Past: Co Dublin 5000 BC–1000 AD' in *Dublin City & County: From Prehistory to Present* (Geography Publications, Dublin)

Turner, Kathleen (1983): *If You Seek Monuments* (Rathmichael Historical Society, Shankill)

Smyth, William J (2006): *Map-making, Landscapes and Memory; A Geography of Colonial and Early Modern Ireland c. 1530-1750* (Cork University Press, Togher, Cork)

Sweeney, Clair L (1991): *The Rivers of Dublin* (Dublin Corporation)